And God ᵤₚₑₗₗ

And God SPOKE

The Authority of the Bible
for the Church Today

Christopher Bryan

A Cowley Publications Book

Lanham, Chicago, New York, Toronto, and Plymouth, UK

A COWLEY PUBLICATIONS BOOK
4501 Forbes Boulevard, Suite 200, Lanham, Maryland 20706
www.rowmanlittlefield.com

Estover Road, Plymouth PL6 7PY, United Kingdom

Library of Congress Cataloging-in-Publication Data
Bryan, Christopher, 1935–
    And God spoke : the authority of the bible for the church today /
    Christopher Bryan.
        p. cm.
    Includes bibliographical references.
    ISBN 1-56101-201-7 (alk. paper)
    1. Bible—Evidences, authority, etc. I. Title.
BS480 .B75 2002
220.1'3—dc21   2001055650

Editor: Cynthia Shattuck; Copyeditor and Designer: Vicki Black
Cover art: Photograph from space of clouds at sunset taken by James
Lovell from the Gemini 7 spacecraft, December 1965.

Printed in the United States of America.

The paper used in this publication meets the minimum requirements of
American National Standard for Information Sciences—Permanence of Paper for
Printed Library Materials, ANSI/NISO Z39.48-1992.

Contents

Acknowledgements

"All books," said someone to me the other day, "and certainly all theological books, are really group efforts." That is certainly true of this one. I have, as always, to thank my friend and colleague James Dunkly, Librarian of the School of Theology of the University of the South, for help at every turn, from providing resources to reading the manuscript at a key phase in its creation. I must thank my friend the Very Reverend James Fenhagen, who likewise read the manuscript, and made some important suggestions. I must thank my research assistant Vicki Burgess, who has done marvelous work in checking the manuscript and preventing me on numerous occasions from making a fool of myself. I must thank my colleagues at the University of the South, and especially in the School of Theology, for much enlightening as well as enjoyable conversation over many years. I must thank our faculty secretary Shawn Horton, who is always willing to meet cheerfully a request for another copy of something, or another document scanned, however awkward or ill timed the request may be. I must thank Cynthia Shattuck and her colleagues at Cowley Publications, whose editorial work, in my opinion, has vastly improved my efforts. Finally, I should note that several chapters of this book build upon papers and editorials that I contributed to the *Sewanee Theological Review* between Pentecost 2000 and Easter 2002. I am grateful to the University of the South for permission to make use of this material.

Christopher Bryan

Making Decisions in the Church

This book began, in a sense, with the 1998 Lambeth Conference—not that I attended it! But I read about it, and I saw the reports on BBC television. These reports presented us with the spectacle of several hundred Anglican bishops, all of them presumably persons of good will and at least average intelligence, claiming to accept the authority of Holy Scripture. Yet they were deeply divided as to what Holy Scripture said on a question that clearly exercised them very much, namely, what the church ought to teach about homosexuality. Should the church still teach that practicing homosexuality is a sin, or can we now discern situations in which it might not be? Could the church bless homosexual unions, or not? Is it possible for persons living in and affirming such relationships to be suitable candidates for ordination, or not? In engaging in these discussions the conference was, of course, engaging a debate that had been taking place in the church for some time, and that, indeed, continues to this day.

What stirred me to write the present book was not the debate itself, important though that undoubtedly was, nor the resolutions to which the conference came, important though those undoubtedly were, but the fact that those on *both* sides of the question have generally claimed that the authority of Holy Scripture, properly understood, supports them. Granted the intelligence and the good will on both sides, one is bound to ask how this can be. How can well-intentioned and intelligent persons come to such opposite conclusions about the same documents? Are the scriptures simply not clear? Are the parties to the debate interpreting the scriptures in different ways? And if so, what is the right way? *Is* there a "right way"? And what of "authority"—a notoriously slippery term? Do both sides mean the same thing by it? And if not (or even if so), what *ought* they to mean? Is there a particular way in which the scriptures can or ought to be authoritative for the church's discourse, and if so, what is it?

As I said earlier, I saw these questions arising from a debate that had taken—and continues to take—an especially poignant form within Anglicanism. Yet those same questions, once raised, evidently apply elsewhere in the church. We have only to consider the different views that have been expressed within the Roman Catholic Church (and not only there) over the ordination of women to the priesthood. In his *Ordinatio Sacerdotalis* (1994), opposing the ordination of women, Pope John Paul II repeatedly appealed to scripture; yet he was doubtless aware that not only Karl Rahner—arguably the leading Roman Catholic theologian of the twentieth century—but even the Pontifical Biblical Institute had already said that they could see scripture pointing in quite different directions. *Mutatis mutandis,* it appears to me that the questions that I have raised with regard to the debate on homosexuality within Anglicanism could be raised here, too.

Given, then, our evident problems in the handling of scripture, is there anything useful we can say on the subject? I think so. We can, to begin with, ask some theoretical questions. What do we actually *believe* about the proper place of scripture in the church? What, if anything, can we infer on the subject from scripture itself? What of various expressions that Christians commonly use of the scriptures—that they involve "revelation," that they are "the Word of God," that they are "inspired"? What do such expressions imply? Even with a term as elusive as "authority," we may reasonably ask whether, among its many possible meanings, there is any particular sense in which, in the present context, it expresses something that we need to say. Then we can go on to consider practical matters. What does a church that takes scriptural authority seriously actually *do* with the Bible? How does such a church handle, study, and pray with the scriptures? And what might be the result of that?

The following is, then, an attempt to formulate what I might have said to the Lambeth bishops had they asked me some of the questions I have outlined above (an unlikely enough scenario, I grant!). It is certainly not an attempt to persuade anyone who does not accept the authority of scripture to do so, although of course I should be pleased if it did that very thing. Rather, this book is addressed to those who already know the authority and inspiration of the Holy Scriptures as a factor in their lives, but wish to reflect further on the nature of that authority and inspiration, and the proper ways to accept and make use of them within the church. We are capable of making idols out of even the greatest of God's gifts. The church, the life of prayer, the sacraments, and the Holy Scriptures—all can be turned into substitutes for the reality to which they should point. And as C. S. Lewis used to say, good things that are made into idols become demons. How then are we to avoid this, yet still take the authority and inspiration of scripture seriously?

PART I

What Do
We Believe?

CHAPTER ONE

Interpreting the Bible

> In Caesarea there was a man named Cornelius, a centurion of the Italian Cohort, as it was called. He was a devout man who feared God with all his household; he gave alms generously to the people and prayed constantly to God. (Acts 10.1–3)

E vidently Cornelius was not afraid to stand out from the crowd. Why, after all, should a centurion be worshipping the God of Israel? What was wrong with the gods of the legions? With Mars? With Mithras? Why choose the god of a conquered nation? Yet that, as we encounter Cornelius in Acts, is exactly what he is doing. And apparently such worship is acceptable to God, for Cornelius' prayer is heard. He is granted a vision, and receives a command: "Send men to Joppa for a certain Simon who is called Peter" (Acts 10.5).

Simon Peter also, as we come upon him, is keeping the third hour of prayer; and Simon Peter is puzzled. He, too, has seen a vision: many creatures, clean and unclean. He has heard a voice: "Get up Peter, kill and eat!" and then,

"What God has made clean, you must not call profane"
(Acts 10.13, 15). What can this mean?
    Messengers arrive from Cornelius to summon Peter,
and he goes with them. The story that follows is well
enough known. Peter enters Cornelius's house, Cornelius
tells of his vision, and Peter realizes that he has learned
from Cornelius something new about the God whom he
serves and proclaims. Here then is something that happens quite often in Holy Scripture when the Word of God
comes to someone outside the people of God and that
person hears and obeys. In such cases the Word invariably
manifests itself as a "corrective" to those within.[1] It comes
as a warning, a roadblock against ways not to be taken.
And to his credit, Peter has the courtesy to admit it—not
something that has always been a mark of Christian mission! "I truly understand that God shows no partiality,
but in every nation anyone who fears him and does what
is right is acceptable to him," he says (Acts 10.34b–35).
This does not, of course, mean that Peter is committed to
some kind of vague theism so that he has nothing to say
to Cornelius. He has a great deal to say, on God's account
if not his own, and he goes on to say it. He preaches the
apostolic gospel—what scholars refer to as the *kerygma* (a
Greek word meaning "proclamation"): that is, he
announces the life, death, and resurrection of Jesus Christ
in such a way as to link them to the fulfillment of God's
promises to Israel in the Old Testament.
    Cornelius and his household believe and, to the
amazement of Peter and his fellow Jews, receive the Holy
Spirit. "Can anyone," Peter asks, "withhold the water for
baptizing these people who have received the Holy Spirit
just as we have?" (Acts 10.47). So Peter promptly has
them baptized—the church, not for the last time in its

history, hastening to ratify what God has obviously already done.

The importance of Cornelius's baptism in Luke's eyes can scarcely be doubted. He describes it, in effect, three times (Acts 10.1–48, 11.4–18, 15.7–9)—as many times as he tells the story of the conversion of Paul. These repetitions are interwoven with other episodes by no means irrelevant to their theme, such as Paul's conversion and the beginning of the gentile mission. So we may justifiably say that the significance of Cornelius's baptism is being reflected in one way or another, implicitly or explicitly, throughout virtually the whole of the middle part of the book of Acts.

The reasons for this fuss were obvious enough to those involved. In baptizing Cornelius, Peter was taking a tremendous risk, and as Luke tells the story, he is soon in hot water for it. "Why did you go to uncircumcised men and eat with them?" (Acts 11.3). And that, of course, was not the half of it. By baptizing them Peter had also admitted them to membership of the people of God. Now if there was one thing about which the scriptures were clear, it was surely this. God's word to Abraham was unambiguous: "Any uncircumcised male who is not circumcised in the flesh of his foreskin shall be cut off from his people; he has broken my covenant" (Genesis 17.14). And had not faithful members of God's people died for their obedience to this command during the persecutions of the Jews recorded in 1 and 2 Maccabees? Nothing, surely, could be clearer than this. It could be argued, therefore, that Peter's action in baptizing the uncircumcised Cornelius contradicted the plain and obvious teaching of Holy Scripture. It made nonsense alike of God's promises to Israel and the deaths of the martyrs.

Yet the church eventually ratified what Peter had done, and the Apostolic Council described by Luke in Acts 15 made clear that baptized gentiles were to have a place in the people of God equal to that of baptized Jews. What then? Did that mean that the scriptures no longer mattered for the young church, or that the Bible no longer had authority in the Christian community? Apparently not, for the Apostolic Council itself was careful to point to other parts of the scripture indicating that in the messianic age God *did* intend the gentiles to be part of God's people (Acts 15.15–18). And in time, of course, Paul would write his Letter to the Romans and show (especially in chapter 11) that the Scriptures from the beginning pointed to what had now happened—indeed, that when properly understood they showed that God had *not* forsaken the promises to Israel, but rather was fulfilling them in a wonderful way that would include the gentiles, too.

No, the story of Cornelius does not show us that the scriptures did not matter for the church or that they did not have authority. It does, however, show us two other things.

The Scriptures are Hard to Interpret

The first thing that the Cornelius story illustrates is that the meaning of Holy Scripture with regard to particular questions is not always easy to understand. Scripture is sometimes difficult to interpret. Our forefathers and foremothers were well aware of this. In the ancient world, Jews, Christians, and pagans would have agreed that sacred texts, *because* they were sacred, were somewhat cryptic and required interpretation—and that interpretation would not be easy. The Ethiopian eunuch whom Philip met on the road between Jerusalem and Gaza seemed to show precisely such an attitude. He was reading a scroll of the prophet Isaiah. "Do you understand what you are reading?" Philip asked. "How can I," the eunuch replied, "unless someone guides me?" (Acts 8.30–31).

The interpretation of a sacred text required, then, the best attention, intelligence, and understanding that one had to offer. It needed, as Paul said, the great Hellenistic virtue of *hupomonē*: that is, patience, steadfastness, stickability (see Romans 15.4). Reading the scriptures as authoritative for the church was not therefore a task for wimps or for those who expected quick or easy answers. This was an attitude that persisted in the subsequent history of God's people. It was manifest, for example, in the four levels of scriptural interpretation envisaged in the Middle Ages by the rabbis, and similarly by Christian scholars who looked for "the four senses" of scripture. (I plan to say more of the "four senses" at a later point in this discussion.) Indeed, such deference is manifest in the entire enterprise that has surrounded the interpretation and understanding of Holy Scripture from the beginning of Christian history to the present. Reformed theologians used sometimes to say of the scriptures that they possessed "clarity" *(perspicuitas),* but they did not mean by that that the scriptures were easy to understand. They meant that the effort to understand the scriptures, if made honestly and faithfully, would always, in the end, bear good fruit.

Yet this deference, this awareness of the sheer difficulty of the texts, is precisely what seems to be missing in some of the discussions of the Bible to which I referred in my prologue. Too often those who find a biblical passage, or even a group of passages, that seem to support their views on a particular subject declare that they have found the "plain meaning" (or some such phrase) of the scriptures—with the implication, of course, that everyone who does not agree with them is ignoring the scriptures, and is probably apostate. The fact is, however, that apparent "plain meanings" of particular passages in the Bible have been used to justify every manner of barbaric horror, including

slavery (Leviticus 25.44–46, Sirach 33.25–33, Philemon, Ephes. 6.5–8, Col. 3.22–4:1, 1 Peter 2.18);

ethnic cleansing (Joshua 6.16–21, 8.1–28);

racism (Nehemiah 13.23–31);

violence toward prisoners of war (Joshua 8.23–29, 1 Sam. 15.7–9, 32–33);

massacre of non-combatant civilians in wartime (Joshua 6:15–21, 8.1–2, 10–23);

indiscriminate slaughter, wholesale destruction of the environment, and cruelty to animals, all in pursuit of a personal vendetta (Judges 14.10–19, 15.1–5);

capital punishment (Esther 6.9–10, 9.1–17);

and the oppression and abuse of women (Genesis 19.1–8, Judges 19.22–24, Eph. 5.22–24, Col. 3.18, 1 Peter 3.1).

Needless to say, when we investigate such "plain meanings" and set them in context within the entire biblical story, invariably they turn out to be not quite so "plain" as they first appeared. By way of example, we might briefly consider the first item in the list above—slavery. There are, as I indicate, a number of passages in both the Old and New Testaments showing that those who wrote them accepted slavery as an institution. Undoubtedly the existence of these passages, with their message, "Slaves, obey your masters," was one reason why some slave owners in the seventeenth century and later did not mind missionaries teaching their slaves to read the Bible, and baptizing them. Pro-slavery preachers before and during the American Civil War regularly appealed to such passages. What the slaves themselves then did with the scriptures is, however, very instructive. Instead of binding themselves by biblical passages that reflected an institutional acceptance of slavery, they turned instead to other passages in the Bible, such as God's word to Pharaoh when the people of Israel were enslaved in Egypt, "Let my people go!" and Paul's words about the implications of the baptismal covenant: "As many of you as were baptized into Christ have clothed yourselves with Christ. There is no longer Jew or Greek, there is no longer slave or free, there is no longer male and female; for all of you are one in Christ Jesus" (Galatians 3.27–28). Passages like these naturally led them to form quite a different view of their slavery from that desired by the slave-owners.

In the long run Christian conscience has, of course, decided that the slaves were right, and no Christian would now defend slavery on the grounds of scripture, *despite* the existence of biblical "pro-slavery" texts. Just why, simply as biblical interpreters, the slaves were correct—and showed themselves, indeed, to be sounder exegetes than the pro-slavery preachers—is itself an important question, and we will be looking at it in a later chapter. For the moment, however, I simply offer this story as a further illustration of the point I am making with regard to the story of Cornelius: the scriptures are sometimes hard to interpret, sometimes involve us in what appear to be contradictions, and therefore require serious engagement.

Are there then any matters about which the scriptures are *not* hard to interpret? Is there nothing that the scriptures make plain? Certainly some would say, "There is not." Most of us have encountered people who are so aware of contradictions, ambiguities, difficulties, and anomalies in the biblical texts that they declare them to be useless as a source of any kind of understanding at all. "You can prove anything and everything from the Bible," as an uncle of mine used to say.

Here a sound theology needs to beware of attack from two directions. We need to beware a naïve belief that thinks it can take a couple of verses of scripture in isolation from their wider context and find there universal moral rules that are to be applied remorselessly in all cases, however complex. We need equally to beware of a naïve skepticism that can see in scripture *only* a mass of contradictions and inconsistencies from which it is possible to prove anything and nothing. On the contrary! There *is* an overall "plain" witness of scripture, and it comes from precisely this "wider context" of which I have just spoken—from scripture taken as a whole, in the light of all its parts and witnesses.

The balance I am trying to strike is illustrated by an exchange in act five of Shakespeare's play *A Midsummer Night's Dream,* between Duke Theseus and Queen Hippolyta. They are speaking of the confused and confusing accounts given by two pairs of young lovers about wonderful, magical things that happened to them in the forest. We, of course, have watched the whole action, and know that, however bemused and confused the lovers are, something wonderful *did* happen to them, and that fundamentally their story is true. Theseus, however, is like a nineteenth-century rationalist critic. He cannot get away

from the contradictions and confusions in the young people's account of their adventure, and therefore sees good
reason to doubt it altogether. He considers their story

> More strange than true. I never may believe
> These antic fables, nor these fairy toys.
> Lovers and madmen have such seething brains,
> Such shaping fantasies, that apprehend
> More than cool reason ever comprehends.

At least, that is the drift of it. Actually, I have done
Theseus a favor (as, incidentally, do many good directors
of the play) because I have cut out a lot of what he says.
Like many nineteenth century rationalist critics he is
somewhat verbose and goes on about his views for a very
long time. But Hippolyta is wiser. She sees the contradictions and confusions in the lovers' stories just as Theseus
does, but she also sees past them to something deeper, an
underlying consistency. So she cuts through Theseus' ver-
biage with five lines that go to the heart of the matter:

> But all the story of the night told over,
> And all their minds transfigur'd so together
> More witnesseth than fancy's images,
> And grows to something of great constancy;
> But howsoever, strange and admirable.

—"admirable," that is, in Shakespeare's (and Hippolyta's)
sense, not merely "something excellent" or "to be
approved of," but something to be *wondered* at—that is,
something wonderful or marvelous. And of course we,
the audience, know that Hippolyta, not Theseus, is right.

That is precisely the way it is with the story of the people of God as told in the scriptures. Whatever the problems and confusions over detail (just *what* was the order

of Jesus' temptations? *was* the Last Supper a Passover, as the Matthew, Mark, and Luke seem to suggest, or was it the night before Passover, as John seems to suggest?); whatever the differences of approach, emphasis, and understanding among the different witnesses (and even within the New Testament, they are considerable—just think of the difference in style and "feel" between John and the other gospels!); whatever the gaps and the omissions that we must either ignore or fill for ourselves (did Isaac *know* what Abraham was going to do? *who* was the young man who, according to Mark, fled naked in Gethsemane?), nevertheless there *is* a thread that binds all, "something of great constancy, but howsoever, strange and admirable." Through the entire collection of texts that we call "the Holy Scriptures" there runs a single story that *anyone* encountering those texts may see—as witness the fact that children's Bibles, from whatever source, invariably follow the same basic narrative outline. It is a story that is foundational to these texts as a collection, and even, we may say, "plain."

What is this story? It is the story of creation and fall, the call of Abraham, the Exodus, Sinai, the settlement, the exile, and the return; it is the subsequent story of the life, death, and resurrection of Jesus Christ for us and for our salvation, of the giving of the Spirit and the foundation of the church, and the future, final presence of Christ as savior and judge. That story is clear. Every single text of the Old Testament relates in some way or other to some aspect of the former part of it. Every single text of the New Testament relates in some way or other to the latter part of it, and, in general, to both parts of it. In particular, texts of the New Testament relate to one event in that story above all others, namely, that God raised Jesus from the dead.

That story is plain and, from the viewpoint of Christian faith and Christian hope, that story is actually the only thing that matters, for it is the story of God's faithfulness. It involves, as Article VI of the Church of England's Articles of Religion expressed it, "all things necessary to salvation." If that story stands, then we stand. If it does not, then we are, as Paul said, "of all people most to be pitied" (1 Corinthians 15.19).

Therefore Christians have called this story *regula fidei,* "the rule of faith."[2] It enshrines the essence of the Christian *kerygma,* or proclamation. It presents us with the apostolic gospel ("gospel," that is, not in the sense of "written gospel," as when we speak of "The Gospel according to Saint Mark," but "gospel" in its original sense, as the evangelists themselves use it, meaning "good news"—the "good news" of Jesus that was proclaimed by the apostles). Faithfulness to this story is the standard by which the apostles themselves exchanged "the right hand of fellowship" (Galatians 2.9; see also 2.2–10). Therefore we must never forget the story, or allow ourselves to be distracted from it. That is why the church insists that we remind ourselves of it by regularly rehearsing it in outline in the creeds. Whenever we begin to feel confused or lost, it is to the foundational story itself, the story of God's faithfulness, that we must return. By studying it and claiming it as ours, we remind ourselves who and whose we are.

Notes

1. Karl Barth, *Church Dogmatics,* G.T. Thompson and Harold Knight, trans. (Edinburgh: Clark, 1956), I.2, 210.

2. See also Note 1 at the conclusion of this book.

CHAPTER TWO

The Church as Witness and Keeper of the Bible

What then are we to make of the contradictions and confusions in the Bible, the differences of approach and emphasis, of which we have spoken? What, to come to the question raised in the Prologue to this book, when persons of intelligence and good will cannot agree as to the meaning of *particular* parts of the Scriptures, or how to live in faithfulness to the gospel? How is the Bible to have authority for us then?

Let us go back to the story of Cornelius. What happens there? It is, under God, the so-called "Apostolic Council" described in Acts 15, the Church gathered in full conclave, that decides what to do—and if we examine the book of Acts as a whole, it is noticeable how Luke, who normally has his characters running all over the place in response to the promptings of the Holy Spirit, at this one point takes great care to show them all coming together to form this council and to discern what may be God's will for the church. This then is the point that I want to make: that it is not just one party, or one group, or one opinion, but the *whole church*, gathered together, that looks at and interprets the scriptures. When a problem arises in the ongoing experience and life of the church it is the church itself—the community of faith, under God—that decides the issue. The church and the church alone is, as Article XX of the Church of England puts it, called to be "a witness and a keeper" of the Holy Scriptures.

What this means in practice was spelled out from within classical Anglicanism by the seventeenth-century divine and bishop William Beveridge. When controversy arises in the church, he says,

> The Scripture itself cannot decide the controversy, for the controversy is concerning itself: the parties engaged in the controversy cannot decide it, for either of them thinks his own opinion to be grounded upon Scripture. Now how can this question be decided better or otherwise than by the whole Church's exposition of the Scripture, which side of the controversy it is for, and which side it is against?[1]

That, essentially, is the model with which Luke already presents us in the book of Acts. Naturally the church does not *create* the truth of God's revelation, but it does interpret it.

Yet this model, too, is hardly without its problems. Is the church capable of the role thus claimed for it? Alone, in its human fallibility, certainly not! Thinking of the entire apostolic ministry, Paul on one occasion asked his Corinthian converts, "Who is sufficient for these things?" (2 Corinthians 2.16), and the implied answer to his ques-

tion was obvious: "No one!" Yet as Paul made clear, there
was more to be said:

> Such is the confidence that we have through Christ
> toward God. Not that we are competent of ourselves to
> claim anything as coming from us; our competence is
> from God, who has made us competent to be ministers
> of a new covenant, not of letter but of spirit; for the let-
> ter kills, but the Spirit gives life. (2 Corinthians 3.4–6)

As I said earlier, it is the church *under* God that must
decide what to do in difficult cases, not the church alone.
We do well to note the form in which the church's decision in Acts 15 is presented: "It has seemed good to the
Holy Spirit and to us" (v. 28). A crucial part of the apostolic gospel is that *to the community of faith is also given
the Holy Spirit, to guide it into all truth* (John 16.12–15;
also 14.26). Every strand of New Testament tradition—
synoptic, Johannine, Pauline, and Petrine—witnesses in
one way or another to that gift and to that promise. That
gift to the church, moreover, is seen in scripture itself as
confirming that it is the church's task to interpret scripture, over against all private interpretations, however
obvious they may seem to the individual interpreter. So
the writer of 2 Peter points out that "no prophecy of
scripture is a matter of one's own interpretation, because
no prophecy ever came by human will, but men and
women moved by the Holy Spirit spoke from God" (2
Peter 1.20–21). We should take note: it is precisely *because*
the scriptures are inspired by Holy Spirit that they are not
subject to individual interpretation, but only to that of
the entire community, to which the Spirit is promised.

From here there are two ways we can proceed, both of
them straightforward and in certain respects understand-

able, neither of them ultimately satisfactory. The first is to say that since God has promised the Spirit to the church, the church in its teachings and actions may be trusted to reflect God's will, and there is nothing for us to worry about. The dangers and temptations of that way are obvious enough. It simply ignores something about which the scriptures themselves are clear—that men and women who are part of the people of God may nonetheless resist the Holy Spirit (see Acts 7:51) and sometimes do. There is, regrettably, no Christian denomination whose history does not contain things for which to be sorry, and none whose duly appointed representatives have not at times made claims that seem now to have been very far from the mind of Christ. Wholesale acceptance of whatever the institutional church does or claims is a kind of idolatry.

The second way is to deny legitimacy to *any* development in Christian tradition after the first generation of the apostles. To that generation the Spirit was given, and to that generation alone. Everything therefore in the century or so after it that deviated from its words and works—such as the evolving structure of the ministry as reflected in the letters of Ignatius, or the evolving church liturgy as witnessed in Justin Martyr—all these works of the second and third Christian generations are to be dismissed. What those who take such a view appear to forget is this: that everything we have that connects us to the first Christian generation, including scripture itself, was transmitted to us *through* those later generations and *by* them. In other words, if the Holy Spirit was not at work in them, then we have no connection at all to the first Christian generation, and no way of knowing what it was or what it stood for. There is such a thing as sawing through the branch on which you are proposing to sit!

Where then does this leave us? It leaves us in a situation that, like the Christian life itself, is often difficult and confusing, but not therefore without hope. I have spoken of the biblical story, the rule of faith. I have described it as a story of the faithfulness of God. Let me state that more precisely. The biblical story is a story wherein God remains faithful, even though we are unfaithful. It is a story wherein God's purposes are fulfilled in spite of and sometimes by way of human recalcitrance, refusal, and stupidity. It is a story wherein the Holy Spirit is promised to guide us into all truth, and that promise is not conditional upon our works.

In fact, the process of the Spirit's guidance throughout the history of the church is precisely what we might have expected, given that propensity of God's people to resist the Spirit to which the Bible repeatedly testifies. That is to say, it is a process that has often been long, slow, and painful, involving false steps, bitter dispute, and deep division, but that seems, nonetheless, in the end to arrive where it ought to arrive. Early discussions over the role of the Law in Christianity involved just such disputes and divisions (see not only Acts 15, but also Galatians 1.6–4.31). Paul's letters indicate other kinds of dispute. In fact, the New Testament itself shows God's people from the beginning squabbling about what it means to be a follower of Jesus and a faithful witness to the gospel, and so it has continued through our bitter debates about Arianism, Apollinarianism, Nestorianism, Eutychianism, and all the rest. The Roman Catholics and the Lutherans have just signed a *Joint Declaration on the Doctrine of Justification* after four hundred years of argument and anathematizing!

Christian faith will then continue to trust the promise that the Holy Spirit will guide God's people into the truth that they need. Yet it will be cautious in assuming that it knows (at least in the short run) precisely where that promise will lead. In matters that divide, where feelings are deep and convictions strong, Christian faith will beware of jumping to quick conclusions on one side or the other. It will, I think, pray always to be delivered from those who point to what they allege is the "plain meaning" of particular passages of scripture (in matters other than the rule of faith), as if they were thereby absolved from every other consideration. One problem is, as we have already said, that when such "plain meanings" are investigated and set in context in the entire biblical story, almost invariably they turn out to be not quite so "plain" as at first appeared. That, however, is not the real point. The real point is that however long or painful the process may be, it is, under God, for the entire church to interpret the Bible and no one else. The church must do this while reflecting upon the scriptures prayerfully in the light of the rule of faith and its teaching office, and that takes time—sometimes even centuries.

The entire church! That very phrase, and the history of Christian squabbling to which I have just pointed, indicates our final problem. I noted earlier how Luke takes great care to show all of the church leaders coming together to form the apostolic council. But where is such unity to be found *now,* among Christian groups who have at times denied each other the right even to call themselves "churches" or "parts of the church"? It is not my task here to speak of the theological significance of Christian division, but since division is a part of our situation, something must be said of our functioning within it.

In a divided Christendom, scriptural interpretation that is faithful will always be ecumenical in its basis and its intention. It will be ecumenical in its basis in that it will ground itself in and always return to the foundational story, the rule of faith, for the rule of faith is one thing that a divided Christendom still has in common. It will be ecumenical in its intention in that it will have an affectionate and caring eye toward the insights and concerns of brothers and sisters in faith who are beyond its particular confessional and denominational boundaries. Indeed, faithful scriptural interpretation will in one sense evolve in deliberate non-cooperation with those boundaries, and a positive non-acceptance of the ultimacy of Christian division. It will do this because it knows very well that it can never be either faithful or scriptural if it ceases to have in mind the fierce irony of Paul's question to the factious Corinthians, "Has Christ been divided?" (1 Corinthians 1:13), and the yearning of Jesus' high priestly prayer according to the Fourth Evangelist:

> I ask not only on behalf of these, but also on behalf of those who will believe in me through their word, that they may all be one. As you, Father are in me and I am in you, may they also maybe in us, so that the world may believe that you have sent me. (John 17.20–21)

Notes

1. *Ecclesia Anglicana Catholica,* on Article VI.

CHAPTER THREE

The Bible as Revelation

There never was a miracle wrought by God to convert an atheist, because the light of nature might have led him to confess a God." So the Elizabethan philosopher Francis Bacon wrote in his Advancement of Learning. But would "the light of nature" do any such thing? What seemed obvious to Bacon has by no means seemed obvious to everyone else. Is God revealed in the world? Is God revealed anywhere? And if so, how? Such questions have occupied philosophers and theologians for generations, and doubtless will continue to do so. The problem of divine revelation is arguably the theological question, not only between religions and within them but also (as Bacon's aphorism implies) between religion itself and atheism. I certainly do not propose to attempt here a history of that debate, but it is important to say where I stand on it, since in what I have been saying so far about Holy Scripture and the authority of Holy Scripture within the church I have been touching on one aspect of it.

First, I am a Christian, which is to say I believe that God has been and is revealed to us through the life and witness of Israel and, supremely, through the life, death, and resurrection of our Lord Jesus Christ. In short, therefore, I affirm both the possibility and the reality of divine self-revelation.

Second, I do not confine the possibility or the reality of that revelation to the Bible or to the church—and I have, among other things, biblical tradition as my warrant for that. According to Genesis, the entire creation is God's utterance. As the psalmist puts it, meditating on the same traditions, "The heavens are telling the glory of God; and the firmament proclaims his handiwork" (Psalm 19.1, compare Romans 1.20). It was therefore in complete faithfulness to scripture that the seventeenth-century priest and mystic Thomas Traherne went so far as to say in his *Centuries of Meditations* that we simply cannot understand the world as it truly is, unless we recognize the voice of God that speaks to us through it:

> You never enjoy the world aright, till you see how a sand exhibiteth the wisdom and power of God, and prize in everything the service which they do to you by manifesting his glory and goodness to your soul, far more than the visible beauty on their surface, or the material services they can do for your body.

Three centuries or so later, we find Thomas Merton making exactly the same point to a group of novices:

> We are living in a world that is absolutely transparent, and God is shining through all the time.... You have to allow the rabbits to be what they are—rabbits. And if you just see that they are rabbits, you suddenly see that they are transparent, and the rabbit-ness of God is shining through in all these darn rabbits![1]

Yet for many reasons, we do not usually experience all creation as revelatory. We do, however, sometimes experience some parts of it in this way. In particular, over the last three thousand years or so, millions and millions of people have so experienced the story of Israel, culminating for Christians in the life, death, and resurrection of Jesus Christ. Those who, in the light of that story, have put their faith in the God of whom the story speaks have also believed that they have, by faith and grace, come to know something of God as God truly is. This particular story is, as I have already pointed out, our foundational story. It is what I referred to in my previous chapter as "the apostolic gospel" and "the rule of faith." It is the story summarized in our creeds.

This story is, of course, much older than the Bible. As the Bible itself makes clear, the Jews were telling what Christians regard as the first part of it—stories of the Exodus, the giving of the Law, and so on—long before the books that enshrine it were written in the form in which we have them, and longer still before those books were assembled into the collection that our Jewish friends call *TANAKH*,[2] or into those similar but by no means identical collections that Christians usually call "the Old Testament." The Jews' telling of that story, and their choice to serve the God who had delivered them from Egypt and made a covenant with them, was what constituted them as God's people, Israel (see, for example, Joshua 24.1–28).

Likewise, the apostles and their followers (as the New Testament makes clear) were proclaiming the gospel story long before the New Testament existed. Sometimes I hear people say something to the effect that they would like the church to get back to "the way it was in New

Testament times." "Fine," I say to them, "but remember: that means you will have to do without the New Testament!" The first Christians had two things—the scriptures of the Old Covenant and the apostolic gospel of Christ crucified and risen—and they understood each in the light of the other. Thus, Paul, writing to the church at Corinth, says, "I handed on to you as of first importance what I in turn had received: that Christ died for our sins in accordance with the scriptures, and that he was buried, and that he was raised on the third day in accordance with the scriptures" (1 Corinthians 15.3–4). That was their story, and that, under God, was what constituted them as God's people, the church.

But then, in time, the various books that were to make up the New Testament were written, either by, or drawing on, the testimony of those who, in Luke's phrase, "were from the beginning eyewitnesses and ministers of the Word" (Luke 1.2). And then, in time (and I mean *quite some time*—centuries, in fact) the church recognized these books as "canonical"—that is, as conforming to her "standard" or "rule" (Greek *kanōn*) and thus truly enshrining and representing her faith.

The story of the development of the Christian canon of scripture is actually quite complicated, and I intend to return to it later. For the moment, suffice it to say that a number of different criteria for recognition as part of the Christian canon are from time to time referred to in the early sources. One such criterion is that some books were regarded as having, directly or indirectly, apostolic authorship. Such was Mark's gospel, whose author, though not an apostle himself, was held to have been "the interpreter of Peter."[3] Another criterion was that a book had been continually used and accepted by the churches.

Thus Augustine of Hippo, while admitting that no one knew who had written the Letter to the Hebrews, nonetheless defended its canonicity because "in any case it is the work of a church writer and it is constantly read in the churches."[4] In these discussions it is clear, nonetheless, that one particular criterion dominates. The texts that came to form the New Testament were chosen above all because they were held truly to enshrine and reflect *the faith that the church already held.* As Augustine put it— and evidently did not regard himself as saying anything very extraordinary—"I would not believe the gospel to be true, unless the authority of the Catholic Church moved me to it."[5]

Above all, of course, the New Testament documents were (and are) witnesses to the apostolic proclamation that God raised Jesus from the dead. This is not to deny that it is possible—and on occasion even useful—to read the New Testament in terms of the plurality of approaches to and understandings of the apostolic gospel that it contains, as when for example we study the particular theology of Paul or the Fourth Evangelist. But the point I am making here is that all the books of the New Testament do, in their different ways and from their different points of view, witness to some aspect or other of the apostolic gospel and the rule of faith, and that witness is the main reason for their place in the canon.

Yet once the church had chosen the texts that witnessed to her faith, it did not then take long before they, among all the many possible and actual modes of witness, were occupying a very special place in her life. Chosen because they reflected her faith, they soon (together with the Old Testament) began to *ground* that faith and in some senses to *govern* it. In other words, the

entire Bible now did for the church what Paul said the
Old Testament did: "Whatever was written in former days
was written for our instruction, so that by steadfastness
and by the encouragement of the scriptures we might
have hope" (Romans 15.4). The nature of that hope for
Christians could, indeed, be described in terms that were
more precise. So the Fourth Evangelist, near to the end of
his gospel, after admitting that he had given us a by-no-
means complete account of everything that Jesus said and
did, went on to make a very significant claim about what
he *had* written: "These things are written so that you may
come to believe [or, may continue to believe][6] that Jesus
is the Messiah, the Son of God, and that believing you
may have life through his name" (John 20.31). In other
words, this book will point you to and enable you to
commit yourself (or to go on committing yourself) to
God's revelation in Jesus Christ, who is the heart and
norm of the apostolic gospel.

That claim is by implication extended, in the church's
understanding, to the rest of the New Testament and to
the whole Bible. Everything significant that was a part of
the original apostolic proclamation—everything therefore that we actually *need*—has been written for us in the
scriptures. Hence the principle of "scripture alone" *(sola
scriptura)*: under God, the church's tradition and her
teaching office have their source and their norm in the
scriptures, and nowhere else. Only here, as Thomas
Aquinas said, is the "proper authority" from which doctrine may argue.[7] Thus, it will be noted, the principle of
"scripture alone," properly understood, implies neither
the rejection of later Christian tradition nor its denigra-
tion, nor the denial of divine revelation apart from Holy
Scripture. Such a denial could only make sense if Holy

Scripture had come into being independently of the life and witness of the continuing church. Simply as a matter of historical fact, that is not what happened. The scriptures were formed and chosen in and by a church that already existed and that already preached with the authority given it by Jesus Christ. The scriptures were selected, as we have seen, as witness to the content of that proclamation.

The expression *sola scriptura* does remind us, however, that the church chose these texts and not others. In *these* texts, the church declared, is God's revelation, the word of faith that we preach. Hence, while in the course of history there are certainly developments in the way in which the church understands the gospel and its implications (such as the change in the last two hundred years in the church's view of slavery), there can be no addition to the content of the gospel itself—to what is "necessary to salvation." To suggest that there could be such an addition is to suggest that the church that recognized the Scripture as witness to the gospel did not in fact know what the gospel was, which would be to undermine both the authority of Scripture and the authority of the church. *Sola scriptura* implies therefore simply what Aquinas said: that *Scripture alone* is the center and norm of our tradition. That is Christian orthodoxy whether Anglican, Orthodox, Protestant, or Roman Catholic.

But we are taking a great deal for granted. Just what *is* "Holy Scripture"? Yes, of course, it is the book we hold in our hands. But what does that mean? Why do we call it not just "God's revelation" or some such phrase, but "scripture"? What, essentially, are "the scriptures"? It is to these questions that we turn next.

Notes

1. Thomas Merton, "Solitude: Breaking the Heart," recorded on Credence Cassettes (Kansas City, Mo.: National Catholic Reporter Publishing Company, DATE).

2. *TANAKH* is an acronym formed from the initial letters of the names of the three parts into which Jewish tradition divides the Bible, namely the Law *(Tora)* the Prophets *(Nebi'im)*, and the Writings *(Ketubim)*. The Law comprises the five books of the Pentateuch. The Prophets are subdivided into the Former Prophets (that is, the historical books of Joshua, Judges, 1 and 2 Samuel, and 1 and 2 Kings) and the Latter Prophets (that is Isaiah, Jeremiah, Ezekiel, and the twelve "minor prophets"). The Writings comprise Psalms, Job, Proverbs, Ruth, Song of Songs, Ecclesiastes, Lamentations, Esther, Daniel, Ezra, Nehemiah, and 1 and 2 Chronicles. This gives a total of twenty-four books, although various combinations are sometimes used to give a total of twenty-two, the number of letters in the Hebrew alphabet. Contemporary Christian writers sometimes refer to the Old Testament as "the Older Testament," and sometimes as "the Hebrew Bible." Neither designation appears to be particularly helpful. The former adds a syllable without, so far as I can see, adding anything significant in the way of sense. The latter is really inappropriate, not least because some portions of the books in question are not in Hebrew at all, but Aramaic (Genesis 31.47; Jeremiah 10.10–11; Ezra 4.8–6.18, 7.12–26; Daniel 2.4–7.28).

3. Papias, cited in Eusebius, *Ecclesiastical History*, 3.39.15.

4. Augustine, *Letters* 129.

5. Augustine, *Contra epistolam Manichaei quam vocant fundamenti*: in Zycho, *Corpus Scriptorum Ecclesiasticorum Latinorum* 25.6.1,197.

6. Both possibilities are represented in the manuscript traditions of John 20.31: see NRSV (contrast text and margin) and NAB (alternative in square brackets).

7. Thomas Aquinas, *Summa theologica* 1, q.1, a.8.

CHAPTER FOUR

The Bible as Text

Let us begin at the beginning. Holy Scripture is a thing written—for that is what the word "scripture" means. The Bible, whatever else it is, is first of all a record of words. It is a text, or, more precisely, a collection of texts. It is therefore what we call "literature." That thought may not be very exciting or glamorous, but it is the unvarnished and undeniable truth, and therefore it is a good place to start. If we believe that God speaks to us through the Bible, then human words, texts, and literature are *how* God has chosen to speak to us, and therefore words, texts, and literature are things that we need to know about.

Everyone, I suppose, acknowledges the truth of this to some extent, even if only implicitly. We recognize that if we are to study the Bible we need—or at least someone in our community needs—to learn the original languages, the Hebrew, the Aramaic, and the Greek, in which its books were written. If no one did that we should have no translations. But there is a great deal more to literature than simply learning a foreign language. What, after all, *is* literature? What are words? And how do they work?

Words are a means—I would argue, our supreme means—of expression. By all other means—facial expressions, gestures, signs, painting, sculpture, and music—I grant that we can express, sometimes very powerfully, emotions and desires. But if we are to refine those expressions, to give more precise information, to explain our feelings, to reflect upon them in any way—for any of those things we need words.

A verse composed by the poet Wordsworth has always amused me:

One impulse from a vernal wood
  May teach you more of man,
Of moral evil and of good,
  Than all the sages can.[1]

To that, my instinct is to reply, "Nonsense!" The fact is, countless impulses from countless vernal woods will not actually *teach* us anything. They may make us *feel* good, but if we want to reflect on that feeling, to consider why we feel like that, or whether we ought to, we need words: which means that we need someone to utter them. We need a sage, maybe, or a poet like Wordsworth, but at any rate we need *someone.* Centuries before the birth of Christ, Isocrates of Athens, the father of rhetorical study, wrote a hymn to the Word in which he declared that speech—the ability to put words together so as to express our emotions, our ideas, our thoughts—was the one ability that really distinguished us from the animals. Speech, he said, was the basis of all progress in law, art, and mechanical invention. It was the only means whereby we could achieve justice, give honor to those who deserved it, or promote civilization and culture.[2] I have yet to see a convincing refutation of those claims.

Words help us to handle our experiences. That, I think, is what we mean when we say to someone, "Oh, thank you! I never heard it put quite like that before." We are saying in effect, "You have made my experience, and what it means, accessible to me in a way that it was not accessible before. I can now articulate it, and therefore draw upon it and use it." That is what great users of words, such as great poets, do for us. In *The Good-Morrow* John Donne said of his relationship to the woman he loved:

> But this all pleasures fancies be.
> If ever any beauty I did see,
> Which I desired, and got, 'twas but a dream of thee.

In doing so, he paid a marvelous compliment to his lady. He also gave all those who have been in love ever since and who come across his words a marvelous way in which to express and understand what *they* feel. And that is only one of the things that great words can do.

So words matter. If Christians, Jews, and Muslims are right to suppose that God has chosen to address them through human words in human literature, making them "peoples of the book," perhaps God's choice is not so surprising, after all.

Four Modes of Language

But we do not always use words in the same way. Indeed, depending on our mood, our situation, and our purpose, we can find ourselves using them in very different ways. The twentieth-century literary critic Northrop Frye usefully divided our ways of using language into four kinds or "modes."[3]

First, he said, is the "descriptive" mode: that is, words in propositions, words used for the purpose of conveying information about something beyond themselves. The manual of instructions that came with my television satellite receiver provides me with many fine examples of that kind of language, such as this:

> The UHF remote sends ultra-high frequency radio signals to a UHF antenna that is connected to the back of the receiver. Because UHF signals travel through solid objects, you can use the remote to control the receiver from another room, or even from another floor in the building, to a possible maximum of 100 feet away from the receiver.

Next we have what Frye called the "conceptual" mode. That is where the truth (or alleged truth) to which the words point is to be found *within the words themselves* and there are constant appeals to reason. Philosophical discourse provides an obvious example of this kind of language—such, for example, as the conversations described in Plato's *Phaedo:*

> "Do not even the poets continually repeat that we neither hear nor see anything accurately? And if these bodily senses are not accurate or dependable, still less likely are the others, all of which are surely inferior to these two. Do you not agree?"
>
> "Certainly," said he.
>
> "Then," said he, "when does the soul grasp truth? For when she attempts any investigation in company with the body, she is obviously deceived by it."
>
> "That is true."
>
> "Is it not by exact reasoning, if at all, that any truth becomes evident to her?"

"Yes."

"And surely she reasons best, when none of these things, neither hearing nor vision, pain nor pleasure, intrudes to vex her?"

Then there is what Frye calls the "ideological" mode of language: that is, words used to appeal not merely to reason, but to our loyalties, to our sense of belonging, to commitments that are prior to our reason and our intelligence and are in some ways more important than they are—as in the speeches of Winston Churchill to the British people during World War II, or Abraham Lincoln's *Gettysburg Address.*

It is rather for us to be here dedicated to the great task remaining before us, that from these honored dead we take increased devotion to that cause for which they here gave the last full measure of devotion; that we here highly resolve that the dead shall not have died in vain, that this nation, under God, shall have a new birth of freedom; and that government of the people, and by the people, and for the people, shall not perish from the earth.

Finally there is the visionary, or, as Frye calls it the "imaginative"[4] mode of language: that is, words used to take us beyond our reason or our loyalties to worlds where our ordinary modes of consciousness are only one possibility among many, where imagination, fantasy, dreams, and intuition have play.

Sit, Jessica: look how the floor of heaven
Is thick inlaid with patines of bright gold:
There's not the smallest orb which thou behold'st
But in his motion like an angel sings,

Still quiring to the young-eyed cherubins;
Such harmony is in immortal souls.[5]

Words used in this last mode can carry us in imagination to other worlds—to the worlds of the gods, of myth, of universes transcending the universe we know. And here we find stories of our relationship to those worlds—stories of creation, fall, and redemption. Here we find those grand, overarching narratives that shape our understanding of the universe around us, and our place in it.

All religions, of course, offer such narratives, and so do all societies and cultures. Think, for example, of the differing assumptions about the nature of the United States involved in the story echoed at the beginning of Lincoln's *Gettysburg Address* ("Four score and seven years ago our fathers brought forth upon this continent a new nation, conceived in liberty, and dedicated to the proposition that all men are created equal"), or in the *rival* stories (for that is what they are) implicit in such notions as "manifest destiny," "Aryan supremacy," or "black power." All of us, whether we like it or not, live out our lives in the light of such stories—even if it is only the story implicit in a conviction that there *is* no story of any ultimate significance, that our lives, our civilizations, and the universe itself are merely the results of a meaningless clash of atoms.

Words in the visionary mode may or may not tell us something that is true about the universe and our relationship to it. What they undoubtedly *do* tell us is something of how we *feel* and *perceive* our relationship to the universe. In other words, they tell us something of ourselves. Hence words in the visionary mode are above all *self*-expressive and *self*-revelatory. In fact they are self-revelatory in ways that few other modes of expression can be. For you to see me, you must stand before me. But when I speak in the visionary mode, if I choose my words right and you are able to hear them, then I can invite you into my heart. I can reveal my inner self to you, my ideas, my beliefs, my hopes, my fears, my desires, and my dreams. No other means of self-disclosure can do that.

The Bible and the Four Modes of Language

The Bible contains all of the modes of language that Frye identified. There is descriptive language, as in the court histories of Saul and David in 1 and 2 Samuel, or the accounts of Paul's journeys in Acts. There is some conceptual language—not much of it, I have to confess, but examples can be found, as when Jesus uses a form of argument that the rabbis called "light and heavy" and that we call *a fortiori:* "If God so clothes the grass of the field, which is alive today and tomorrow is thrown into the oven, will he not much more clothe you—you of little faith?" (Matthew 6.30). Ideological language abounds, as in the prophets' calls for repentance and faithfulness to the God of Israel. And there is visionary, or imaginative, language, evident in passages such as the accounts of creation in Genesis, in John's account of the incarnation of the Word, or the visions of the book of Revelation.

It is, however, this last kind of language—the visionary—that is evidently the most significant and even, we may say, *normative* for these particular texts. Behind biblical descriptions, behind biblical discourse, and even behind biblical appeals to our loyalties, there is *always* the vision, a fundamental awareness of some aspect of the biblical story, and of the part to be played in that story by those addressed. In other words, it is always the guiding narrative—the *mythos,* the myth—that provides the biblical view of the universe, and hence guides its rhetoric, its appeals to our loyalties, its logic, and even its choices of what to describe. This guiding narrative we have already identified in other connections: it is the story of creation, covenant, and redemption; it is the "rule of faith." That (in Queen Hippolyta's phrase) is the "something of great constancy" that binds all together. Identifying this story is not in itself a matter of faith. On the contrary, that this story governs the collection of texts that we call the Bible is, I would claim, a clearly demonstrable feature of the Bible when it is simply taken seriously as literature.

I have just referred to the central story to which the scriptures testify as their "myth." In speaking thus, I hope it will be understood that I do not accept the vulgar twentieth century prejudice that equates "myth"—and also, incidentally, "story," "fable," "poetry," "imagination," and "fiction"—with "falsehood." On the contrary, to describe something as "myth," in the sense in which I am using the word, is to speak of the way in which it functions in relation to our consciousness. It is to say nothing whatever of the reality of the matters with which it deals, or the value of its manner of dealing with them. When we examine the biblical text we notice that the subjects of its myth are, indeed, broadly similar to those that occupy the myths of other religions and cultures—the subjects of creation, fall, redemption, death, judgment, hope, and so on. The early theologians of the church used to say that this was because in other religions the demons had counterfeited true religion. We may say, rather more positively, with Karl Barth, that "all human activity is a cry for forgiveness"[6]—and see in all these different myths, with their gleams of hope, elements in that cry. But still that does not mean that we regard all myths as equally true or equally valuable.

Notes

1. William Wordsworth, *The Tables Turned.*

2. Isocrates, *Antidosis* 253-57.

3. Northrop Frye, *Words with Power: Being a Second Study of "The Bible and Literature"* (San Diego: Harcourt, Brace, Jovanovich, 1990), 4–29.

4. "Imaginative" is fine: I avoid that word only because of the common prejudice against "imagination" to which I shall be referring later in this chapter.

5. William Shakespeare, *The Merchant of Venice* 4.1.54-63.

6. Karl Barth, *The Epistle to the Romans,* trans. Edwyn C. Hoskyns (London: Oxford University Press, 1933), 96 97.

CHAPTER FIVE

The Bible as a Book of Meeting

We have observed that the normative language of the Bible is neither descriptive, nor conceptual, nor ideological, but visionary—that is, self-revelatory. What then if God has chosen to address us through the Bible? In that case we must say that the manner in which God has chosen to address us is likewise normatively neither descriptive, nor conceptual, nor ideological, but self-revelatory. We are saying that through scripture God invites us into God's heart. No one has expressed this better than Archbishop William Temple in the preface to his *Readings in St. John's Gospel:*

> The Word of God does not consist of printed propositions; it is living; it is personal; it is Jesus Christ. That living Word of God speaks to us through the printed words of Scripture; and all our study of those printed words helps us to receive it. But the point of vital importance is the utterance of the Divine Word to the soul, the self-communication of the Father to his children.[1]

Therefore if we use the scriptures rightly, we will come to them not looking in general to hear something described or to learn regulations, but to be exposed to the living God. Moses had a "tent of meeting," a place of encounter. As Sandra M. Schneiders has powerfully expressed it, the Bible is the Word of God for us because it is such a place, a tent of meeting, a book of meeting, a text of meeting— because God wills not merely to be known *about*, but to be *known*, "face to face," as the Lord knew Moses (Deuteronomy 34.10).[2]

This is the point made by the book of Job, at the end of which we learn that only Job, who has expressed enormous anger with God, has actually spoken "what is right" about God, or is truly God's "servant" (Job 42.7). At first sight this is very surprising, for all the other characters in the book have attempted by their words and their logic to defend God's honor. The difference, however, is this: all those others have attempted to defend God's honor by talking *about* God. Job, at his angriest, has repeatedly turned back and addressed himself *to* God (6.11-21, 10.2-21, 13.20-14.22, 30.20-31). Only Job, even in his rage, has actually sought to hear and encounter God:

> Oh, that I knew where I might find him,
>   that I might come even to his dwelling!
> I would lay my case before him,
>   and fill my mouth with arguments.
> I would learn what he would answer me,
>   and understand what he would say to me....
> I cry to thee, and thou dost not answer me,
>   I stand, and thou dost not heed me (23.3-5, 30.20).

This encounter is what Job desires, and this, in the end, is what is given him. It is entirely beside the point that to those of us who watch the scene (as do Job's friends) from outside, it seems that when God speaks the words are, as the novelist Louis de Bernières puts it, "magnificently irrelevant," and that, in effect, Job wins the argument.[3] For this is not about winning arguments. It is about the presence or absence of God: and apparently for Job, who in this case is the only one qualified to judge, God's words and God's presence are enough:

> I had heard of you with my ears;
> but now my eyes have seen you. (42.5)

This satisfaction with the mere *presence* of God is always the way it is with God's saints and God's prophets, however baffling that may be to the rest of us. Even our Lord's final cry of desolation upon the cross does not center upon his own agony, but upon *the apparent absence of God*.

It is, then, a fundamental mistake to come to the Bible looking merely for descriptions, propositions, or instructions. We are to come in search of a relationship, and we can never truly understand these texts unless we do. Such a relationship is, of course, risky. Propositions and descriptions may instruct or inform us. Relationships, if we let them, transform us. Propositions and descriptions we can grasp, and sometimes we may get them right, but another self cannot be grasped. Another self is always a mystery, always a source of new possibility, new challenges, and new joy. Even a human self is that, indeed, even a beloved beast—a dog, a cat, or a bird—and certainly the "Self" that is Almighty God.

If the foregoing is correct, then it prepares us to go on to something else. Self-revelation is by its nature *to* someone. Meetings and encounters are always between selves. Therefore self-revelation always involves at least two, and both of them affect it. You may say to me, "I love you," and perhaps you mean it. But what I hear by that will depend on a host of things—notably, whatever may have been my past experiences of what was called "love." You may say to me, "I want to give you a gift." But I, perhaps, have always experienced gifts as means by which people have tried to take me over, to manipulate me, to control me. What then do I hear? Not your gift to me at all, but words expressing a threat, the danger of being led where I cannot or do not wish to go.

Hence you and I may listen to the same words on the same occasion, but the chances are we shall each learn something different from them, because we are not the same person. If the words are about something fairly limited in scope or significance, something merely descriptive, like the distance from Rome to Naples, the difference may not matter much. But if they are about something more complex—a personal self-disclosure, a call that arouses our emotions or challenges our commitments—then the difference may be very great indeed. That is something, I think, that the postmodernists and the deconstructionists, for all their excesses in some directions, have usefully reminded us about in the course of the last fifty or so years. Our understanding of any communication is to some extent qualified by who we are and what we bring to it.

Shakespeare, of course, knew that perfectly well. It is precisely the assumption that lies behind the players' scene in act two of *Hamlet:* the reactions of a guilty man to the scene of murder enacted before him will be different from those of an innocent. But that, perhaps, was because Shakespeare was a man of the theater, and nothing can make clearer to you than the theater that communication involves two sides. The producer and the actors may think their play is the most seriously tragic thing ever done. But if the audience laughs, then it is funny, at least for that performance, and that is that.

What does all this mean with regard to God's self-disclosure in the Bible? Think of Jesus' parables—and the approach to them for which he calls: "Let anyone with ears to hear listen!" What, for example, does the parable of the lost sheep *mean*? If I think of myself as a shepherd it will, I think, mean one thing. But if I think of myself as a sheep, then it may mean something quite different. I choose this example advisedly, because this particular parable appears twice in the synoptic gospels—in Luke 15 and Matthew 18—and the difference in understanding that I have suggested is actually implied by the two settings. It is clear that in Matthew the hearers are being invited to think of themselves as sharing the responsibility for all God's sheep. In Luke, it is evident that what is at issue is the universality of grace, even toward those who have strayed. What does this mean for our understanding of parables generally? It means that to some extent the meaning of the parable has to be its meaning for us, or even, sometimes, for *me*. We have to decide. We have to *interpret*.

Am I then saying that texts in general, or inspired texts in particular, can mean anything? No. That is what some postmodernists claim, but it is not what I am saying. Even in the personal encounter described above, I would do well, before rejecting or criticizing your gift, at least to try to discover what you meant by it, and whether my fears of it were justified. Do you seem to be a manipulative sort of person? How do other people find you? What information can I get that will help me make a judgment? The same is certainly true of our approaches to the Bible. One value of ordinary, critical biblical scholarship—that is, treating our texts as texts, with the best historical, linguistic, and literary understanding we can obtain of them—is that it affords us a measure of defense (I do not say a complete defense) against interpretations that simply indulge our fantasies, our fears, or our desires. Think again of the parable of the lost sheep. What does it mean? As we have noted, it may mean something different depending on whether you think of yourself as a sheep or as a shepherd. But what if you insist that the text is an advertisement for good fencing? Then, I think, decent research into the nature of these texts and their background will supply us with enough information to declare simply that you are wrong. How do we know that? Because we have access to a mass of information about the way parables were used and understood by Jewish teachers, about economic and social conditions in the world of Jesus, that rules out such an interpretation.

So serious study, to whatever degree it is possible for us, is important if we are properly to encounter the scriptures. We owe them that. Yet the more significant point I am trying to make here is that when we attempt to disclose ourselves to one another, we run the risk of being misunderstood and even rejected. Which of us who has ever risked self-disclosure to another does not know that? And the final significance—indeed the quite awesome significance—of talk about God's self-disclosure to us is that it naturally implies that even God runs precisely the same risk. If the story of the annunciation to Mary is not simply the account of a largely meaningless ritual, then at its heart lies the fact that our Lady was free. She could have said, "No!" And for whatever time there was (perhaps the merest fraction of a second) between the angelic salutation and her response, Heaven's own purposes hung in the balance.

Much of the Bible is, in fact, about humanity saying, "No!" to God, and God enduring that rejection. That, for example, is what the creation story in Genesis describes. God offers to humankind all the fruit of the garden, all the possibilities of human existence. God's own knowledge of good and evil is, of course, *not* a possibility of human existence: so God warns the Adam (humankind) against seeking it, and that warning, too, is a gift. But rather than accept God's gifts as acts of generosity intended for their joy, the man and the woman choose to accept the serpent's assurance that God has an ulterior motive: God's gifts have something sinister behind them, and God's warnings about human possibilities and impossibilities are false. "You will not die; for God knows that when you eat of it your eyes will be opened, and you will be like God, knowing good and evil" (Genesis 3.4-5). So they prefer the word of a snake to the word of God, and seek the impossible knowledge. And not only they, but also God, must endure the result.

Jesus' parable of the talents reflects a similar message. The kingdom of heaven is compared to a man going on a journey. He entrusts his property to his servants so that they may trade with it and increase his investment for him. But one of the servants simply digs a hole in the ground and hides his talent there. Why? On the day of accounting he says to his master, "I knew that you were a harsh man, reaping where you did not sow, and gathering where you did not scatter seed; so I was afraid, and I went and hid your talent in the ground" (Matthew 25.24-25). But how did the servant "know" this? The other servants appear to have "known" nothing of the kind. They just went and did as they were told. Evidently the third servant brought his "knowledge" with him. As Daniel Otto Via pointed out some years ago, the third servant's image of the master was what locked him in his fear and so deprived him of the chance to be what he could have been. "The servant was paralyzed, not because he was in a victimizing context, but because he chose to understand himself as a victim"[4]—and, we might add, to understand his master as an oppressor. What is more, both he and his master were obliged to live with the consequences.

Undoubtedly, however, the supreme vision of the risk that God takes in self-disclosure appears in the cross. Jesus said "Do not throw your pearls before swine, lest they trample them under foot and turn to attack you" (Matthew 7.6). Yet that, in a sense, is exactly what Jesus did do, and it is what God does, all the time. The cross is one result of that generosity. "He saved others, he cannot save himself!" (Mark 15.31) Of course that is not the only thing to be said about the cross. The cross is God's own act as God comes to find and rescue us in the midst of sin and death. The cross is God's choice to endure with us the results of our stupidity and disobedience. The cross is the work of God who is *Immanuel*, that is, God-with-us. But that the cross is also a sign of the risk God takes for us in self-disclosure is certainly one thing to be said about it, and not the least important.

What then does it mean when we say that God speaks to us through Holy Scripture? It means that God has accepted the risk of being revealed to us through words, through texts, through literary genres, through the weaknesses and fallibilities of human authors, the errors of scribes and translators, and all the flaws, fallacies, and fantasies of human speaking and human hearing. It means the willing vulnerability of God who here and now, in the pages of a book I can hold in my hands, as in the blessed sacrament, as in Mary's arms in Bethlehem, as before the Sanhedrin and on Calvary, does not think Godhead a thing to be exploited, but humbles himself, being obedient in all things, even to death on a cross (compare Philippians 2.5-11). It means what our fathers and mothers in faith called *condescensio Dei*, the marvelous "condescension of God"—the act of one who deliberately abandons power and privilege, in order to identify with the weak and the deprived.

Nevertheless—and how important that biblical "nevertheless" always is!—nevertheless, this same Bible also tells us that God raised Jesus from the dead, and through our baptism promises to raise us, if we will have it so. And *that* means that this same God will not allow even stupidity, overconfidence, and disobedience as great as ours to have the last word, unless we insist on it.

Notes

1. William Temple, *Readings in St. John's Gospel*, first and second series (London: Macmillan, 1939), ix.

2. Sandra M. Schneiders, *The Revelatory Text: Interpreting the New Testament as Sacred Scripture*, second edition (Collegeville, Minn.: The Liturgical Press, 1999), xix.

3. *The Book of Job*, with an introduction by Louis de Bernières (Edinburgh: Canongate, 1998), xiii. De Bernières's own "anti-God" statement would, in its fervor, be worthy of Job himself, were it not

that Bernières falls into the same trap as Job's friends: he talks *about* God, never *to* God (see xiii-xiv)!

4. Daniel Otto Via, *The Parables: Their Literary and Existential Dimension* (Philadelphia: Fortress, 1967), 119.

CHAPTER SIX

The Bible as the Word of God

In view of all that we have said of the scriptures so far, it is perhaps not surprising that people have regularly spoken of them as God's own word—"the Word of God." Nevertheless, that expression is not without difficulties of its own, and at this point I should like briefly to examine them.

The major problem is, I believe, encapsulated in a conversation that took place recently between one of my students and his canonical examiner. "Surely," the student said, "Jesus is the only true Word of God?" "No," the examiner said, "Scripture is the true Word of God." They argued, but did not get far. I am not surprised. In my opinion, they were both (as William Temple used to say) right about what they were affirming, and wrong about what they were denying. More important, they were forgetting that, like all our language about God, the expression "the Word of God" is what theologians since Thomas Aquinas have referred to as *analogy,* and what literary critics in general and biblical critics in particular call *metaphor*. Since in the present discussion I am moving largely in the field of literary and biblical criticism, I shall use the latter term, metaphor.[1]

In the third act of Shakespeare's play *Macbeth*, after Macbeth has committed several murders, he says,

> I am in blood
> Stepp'd in so far, that should I wade no more,
> Returning were as tedious as go o'er.

That is a wonderful metaphor. Of course what it says is not true: Macbeth is not up to his knees in human gore. He is standing on the stage in front of us, and we can see that he is not. Yet it remains a marvelous way of describing his situation. It expresses perfectly his consciousness of having committed so many murders, of having so much blood on his hands (as we say—that, of course, is another metaphor) that he can never repent, never find a way out of his crimes, but rather must add crime to crime. It expresses all that. Indeed (as any fool can see) it expresses it all far *better* than that (or any) prosy description of his situation could ever do. Yet, as I have said, it is not, actually, true. And that is always the case with the metaphor. It conveys to us truths that cannot be so well conveyed by any other means; and it does so by saying something that is manifestly false, by a juxtaposition that is plainly unrealistic.

I hope that it is clear from what I have already said (and that it will become even clearer from what I will go on to say) that I am not using the word metaphor as it is sometimes used to speak of mere trope or verbal flourish. I regard metaphor as a real means of communication leading to real knowledge about real things. When Paul tells the Colossians that God "has rescued us from the power of darkness and transferred us into the kingdom of his beloved Son" (1.13), he is using metaphor: not because he believes that the things of which he speaks are not real, nor because they are real only as descriptions of his or the Colossians' state of mind, but because they are, in a sense, *too* real to be spoken of adequately in ordinary descriptive discourse.

There are two ways in which metaphors can lose their power to work as metaphor. The first way is when they become what we call "dead" metaphors. This is what happens when a metaphor is so successful and so commonly adopted that we go on using it, and even, in a sense, "understanding" it, long after we have forgotten what were the real elements that it originally identified. For example, most people know perfectly well what is meant when we describe something as a "flash in the pan." In my experience, however, comparatively few people know what the metaphor was originally about and most seem to think it had something to do with panning for gold. In fact, it was a metaphor based on the operation of early firearms, and referred to an explosion of gunpowder without any communication beyond the touchhole—in other words, something that initially looked quite impressive, but did not actually discharge any shot. As such, it was a perfect metaphor for any kind of abortive effort that made a lot of fuss, but did not in the event achieve much. Evidently our use of this expression has long survived our knowledge of its origin, and it constitutes what is therefore known as a dead metaphor. Little harm, so far as I know, is caused by this phenomenon.

The second way in which metaphors can cease to operate as metaphors is when they begin to be taken literally—so that the element of obvious untruth (which is, as we have said, of the essence of metaphor) is forgotten. This is especially likely to happen to very powerful and effective metaphors expressing something that is very important to us—what are sometimes called "root" metaphors. When this happens, it is much more dangerous and confusing than the phenomenon of the dead metaphor, because it means that what began as illuminating can actually lead us to complete nonsense—as if we insisted, against all evidence or common sense, that there really *must* be some blood washing around Macbeth's knees and started to look for traces of it. As I have said, this tends to happen to very powerful and important metaphors.

One such powerful metaphor is represented by the daring step taken by some among the prophets of the Old Testament who first called God "Father." This was a bold and enlightening way to describe God's relationship to God's people. Particularly, it could speak of God's faithfulness and God's compassion, as when the prophet prayed,

> For you are our father,
>> though Abraham does not know us
>> and Israel does not acknowledge us;
> you, O LORD, are our father;
> our Redeemer from of old is your name. (Isaiah 63.16)

But what happens if the metaphor is taken literally? Then something very dangerous and misleading happens: our understanding of God, the God of Israel, the God of the whole earth, far from being explicated by the notion "father," is now limited to it. If God is father, we suggest, then God cannot be mother. Fathers are male, so God must be male. And so on. It is as if the Pauline usage were reversed. Far from it being the case that God is "the Father, from whom every family in heaven and on earth takes its name" (Ephesians 3.14–15), God, on the contrary, now takes *his* name from the fatherhood of earth, being defined and limited by it. What place then for Julian of Norwich's vision "that God rejoices that he is our Father, and God rejoices that he is our Mother, and God rejoices that he is our true spouse, and that our soul is his beloved wife"?[2] Evidently, none at all!

Since there can never be a one-to-one relationship between God and any humanly comprehensible language about God, it follows that all language about God must be metaphorical. So with the expression, "the Word of God." This also is a metaphor, whether it is applied to Jesus Christ or to the scriptures. Whatever truth it conveys, it conveys by means of an expression that is true but also in some sense *not true*. Here the "not true" is obvious enough. Your words and mine are sounds uttered by us with our human throats. God is evidently not limited in that way. But that said, words *are* a way in which we reveal ourselves. So, first and obviously, to speak of something as "God's Word" is to claim that through it God has chosen to be revealed, and that is no small claim.

So is Jesus the Word of God? Or is the Bible the Word of God? Or perhaps the sermon at the Holy Eucharist last Sunday was the Word of God? If we believe that God has been revealed to us in Jesus, if we believe that God has been revealed to us through the Bible, and even if we believe that God was revealed to us through the sermon last Sunday, then the answer is "Yes!" to *all* these questions. There is no need for us to argue about it. Metaphors are the most unfussy things in the world, and are happy to fit in wherever they can be useful. As any decent Elizabethan poet could have told us, just because my beloved's cheeks are damask roses, there is not the least reason in the world why your beloved's cheeks may not be damask roses too.

Notes

1. I am aware, of course, that "analogy" is the more comprehensive term, which is why theologians speaking in a general way of what we may say or know about God normally use it. Thus they point out that the creation offers us "images" of God, which both resemble and do not resemble the Creator; or, as Martin Luther put it, that the creatures are "masks," behind which God hides but through which God also speaks.

2. Julian of Norwich, *Showings*, trans. Edmund Colledge and James Walsh (New York: Paulist, 1978), 279.

CHAPTER SEVEN

The Bible as Inspired

We have said that God's Word, God's own self-revelation, comes to us in the Holy Scriptures—and so the scriptures are authoritative within the church. But we may then be moved to ask, "*How* does the Word of God come to us through the scriptures? How does this marvelous thing come about?" The church's answer has long been, "It comes about because God inspires the Holy Scriptures—that is to say, it comes about through the grace and gift of God's own special influence upon them."

The New Testament itself affirms this. As the writer of the second letter of Peter says, "No prophecy of scripture is a matter of one's own interpretation, because no prophecy ever came by human will, but men and women moved by the Holy Spirit spoke from God" (1.20–21). Similarly, the writer of the second letter to Timothy notes that "all scripture is inspired by God and is useful for teaching, for reproof, for correction, and for training in righteousness" (3.16). The writers of these letters were, of course, speaking directly of the Old Testament, but by natural extension the church has applied what they said to the New Testament as well.

All of that might seem simple enough. But there is nothing that the human mind cannot complicate or question. So, for example, there have been a long debates in the history of Christian theology as to how inspiration actually works. Where, for example, should we locate it? Is it to be seen in the ways in which God influences the authors of the texts—which is, perhaps, what the passage from 2 Peter seems to suggest? Or is it in the way in which God influences the texts themselves, as perhaps implied by the 2 Timothy passage? Another aspect of the debate has been concerned with what, in any case, inspiration means for practical purposes. What, actually, are its effects? What does it *do*?

In discussing these matters I think it important first to remind ourselves that when we speak of the Scriptures as "inspired" we are making an affirmation of faith, similar to the kind of affirmation we make when we say that God created the universe, or that God was in Jesus Christ, or that Christ is present in the Blessed Sacrament. That is to say, in all these cases we are presented with an empirical reality—the created universe, the man Jesus, the bread and wine—that *can* be explained and experienced without any reference to God at all, as it is by many people. As the writer to the Hebrews says of the entire apostolic proclamation: "You have not come to something that can be touched" (12.18a). You can examine the bread and wine of the sacrament any way you like: you will never succeed in identifying conclusively the "Christ" part. So it is with Jesus. So it is with the universe. And so it is with the inspiration of Scripture.

Human beings wrote the Scriptures. The formation of the entire collection was, as the Anglican biblical scholar Brooke Foss Westcott put it well over a century ago, "according to natural laws."[1] That is to say, there is in principle a humanly comprehensible and demonstrable explanation for everything in them. We do not, of course, have access in every case to the information that would provide us with that explanation, but in general terms we know what kind of information it would be, and we know the kinds of condition that, if satisfied, would convince us that we had it.

Yet, just as when I say that God created the universe I affirm *by faith* that everything in it is ultimately grounded in and revelatory of God; just as when I say that Jesus is truly God and truly human I affirm *by faith* that through his words and works as we have received them he uniquely discloses the self-giving and self-disclosing will of God, and is therefore divine; just as when I say that Christ is present in the sacrament I affirm *by faith* that the sacrament is an outward and visible sign of inward and spiritual grace given by God to us:

So, when I say that the Scriptures are inspired, I affirm *by faith* that the Scriptures are influenced by God in a special way so as to be, among all human writings, uniquely revelatory of God.

All the forgoing are faith statements, in that they speak of something that may be understood in that way, but does not have to be. They therefore differ from, say, philosophical or scientific statements, which can in principle be demonstrated. Faith statements are more like appreciating beauty, or falling in love, but as we know (or ought to know) nonetheless real and important for that.

To speak of the Bible as "inspired" is then to speak of it, *by faith*, as uniquely God's book, the Spirit's book.

But if there is one thing we can be sure of, it is that where the Spirit of the Lord is, there is freedom. The Spirit blows where it chooses, but we do not know where it comes from or where it goes. Will we then presume to identify in these texts a place for God to work? Will we insist on a particular way of working for the One whom heaven and the heaven of heavens cannot contain? Robert Jenson points out to us the paradox involved in all our notions of inspiration—and its solution. Just how, he asks, can the centuries old writings of a long dead civil servant in the Jerusalem royal court, writings that were in part cribbed from pagan Egyptian models (as, for example, were Proverbs 22.17-24.22), be God's 'wisdom' for our lives in the twenty-first century?

> Not because the Spirit provided exactly the words he one day wrote, thereby guaranteeing their wisdom and power independently of all subsequent history. Rather, because the whole event, from that civil servant's memorizing Egyptian and other wise maxims in his youth to his rethinking them again in maturity, to the accidents of collecting and editing and preserving, to the way in which we attend to the Old Testament reading some Sunday morning, is drawn on by the Spirit's freedom.[2]

Exactly! If the Bible is the Spirit's book, then the Spirit does with the Bible what the Spirit wills within the community of faith to which the Spirit is promised, just as the author of the second letter of Peter says.

If then, to return to the former of two questions that I raised earlier, you were to ask me where we should locate inspiration, I would answer, "Everywhere in the whole process!" Inspiration is to be seen in the original experiences and vision that provoked the writers to write. It is in their calling to write, and their skills as writers. It is to be seen in the work of copyists and scribes, as well as in the discussions and thoughts of early theologians who determined that these texts were canonical. It is in the discussions and thoughts of theologians and exegetes ever since. Inspiration is at work in the work of modern translators and textual critics, and after they have done their work inspiration continues, right down to what goes on with you or me in that moment that we read or hear the Bible and are moved in response to attempt lives of faith and obedience, forgiving and forbearing one another as God for Christ's sake has forgiven us, clothing the naked, feeding the hungry, doing justice and loving mercy. That—all of that!—is the locus of divine inspiration.

What of the second, and perhaps more important question? What, actually, is the result of inspiration? What does inspiration *do* for the Bible? For this, too, the church has long had an answer. In effect it is this: "Because God inspires the Bible, the Bible does not err." Pope Clement VI stated the essence of the matter as early as the fourteenth century. In a letter to the patriarch of the Armenian Church he said that one could be truly Christian only if one believed (*si credisti et credis*) "the undoubted truth (*veritatem indubiam*)" contained throughout all the books of the Old and New Testaments.[3] The particular value of this assertion lies, I think, in its making clear that biblical inerrancy, like the inspiration upon which it depends, is a matter of *faith*. It is not something that can be proved.

Nevertheless, belief in the Bible's inerrancy, like belief in inspiration, is hardly without its problems. The most obvious of these is that in response to Clement, the

Armenians might have asked what many have asked since, "I must believe that the Bible contains undoubted truth about *what?* Undoubted truth about *anything?* Or undoubted truth about matters of faith?"

The best contemporary statement on this question of which I am aware is one that was made after much debate and revision by the Second Vatican Council of the Roman Catholic Church. This asserts that, "the books of Scripture, firmly, faithfully, and without error teach that truth which God, for the sake of our salvation, wished to see confided to the sacred Scriptures."[4] Despite the attempts of some commentators to make more of this than it says, it is evident that the Council as a whole expressed a clear awareness that there are errors and contradictions in the Scriptural records. As Cardinal König pointed out to the Council (and was not challenged), biblical study "shows that the sacred books are sometimes deficient in accuracy as regards both historical and scientific matters."[5] Thus, for example, according to Mark 2.26, David entered the Temple and ate the bread of the presence when Abiathar was high priest; but according to 1 Sam. 21.1-7 it was when Abiathar's father Abimelech was high priest. According to Matthew 27.9, Judas' death fulfilled a prophecy made by Jeremiah, but the verse cited appears actually to be from Zechariah 11.13. And so on.

The focus when the church speaks of "Scriptural inerrancy" is therefore neither upon details of fact or memory, nor upon the types of literature involved in the Bible, but upon the Bible's *purpose*, a purpose that is manifestly not historical or conceptual or literary or scientific, but "for the sake of our salvation." That is to say (and as we have repeatedly noticed) the Bible is what it is for no other reason than that *it enshrines and witnesses to*

the Rule of Faith, through which God chooses to be known.
Biblical inerrancy—the sense in which the Scriptures
cannot be "annulled" or "set aside" (John 11.35)—does
not lie in some supposed incapability of error on the part
either of its human authors or its copyists, but in the fact
that through the Scriptures, for all their human fallibility
("warts and all," as we say) God nevertheless unerringly
tells us what we need to know of Jesus Christ, the divine
grace, and God's calling us to obedience and faith. As for
the warts—it is with the Scriptures as Saint Paul said it
was with the entire apostolic ministry: "we hold this
treasure in earthen vessels, that the surpassing power may
be of God and not from us" (2 Corinthians 4.7).

This leads to a further point: since God has chosen to
inspire the Scripture and to guide it, warts and all, we for
our part are absolved from trying to distinguish between
the "truly inspired" parts of the Bible and the "less
inspired," or between the errant parts and the inerrant.
Still less are we to imagine that by means of such distinc-
tions we can create for ourselves encounters with the genuine Word of God. A rubric in the American *Book of
Common Prayer* (1979) permits the reader at the daily
office to say either "The Word of the Lord" or "Here ends
the Lesson (Reading)" at the end of each of the appointed lessons from Scripture.[6] I often hear that permission
used as a way to express what is clearly an opinion
(whose? the reader's? the parish priest's? the congrega-
tion's?) as to whether what has just been heard was "really" an encounter with God's Word or not. It should not be
used in that way. Such decisions involve a judgment that
we are neither required nor permitted to make. To put it
another way, if God is not embarrassed by the fallibility
of the human words of the Bible, by their historic and sci-

entific inaccuracies and their theological contradictions, but has adapted and made use of them in their fallibility, we do not need to be embarrassed by them either. No doubt in God's eyes even what seem to us the noblest and most sublime parts of Scripture are scarcely less inadequate for the glory to which they witness than what seem to us the most barbaric and politically incorrect. Paul would claim no more for himself than that "we know only in part and we prophesy only in part" (1 Cor. 13.9). Nevertheless, as the writer to the Hebrews pointed out, it is through just such partial and imperfect witnesses and prophets that God has chosen to speak (see Hebrews 1.1).

So much may be said for what I regard as the orthodox and biblical view of biblical inerrancy: to follow the main argument of this book, you may perfectly well skip over the rest of this chapter, and move straight on to the next. I am aware, however, that the phrase "biblical inerrancy" is commonly used (particularly among some evangelical Christians, but not only by them) to imply a good deal more than I have said about the reliability of the Scriptures in matters pertaining to our salvation. According to one such writer, "Inerrancy means that when all the facts are known, the Scriptures in their original autographs and properly interpreted will be shown to be wholly true in everything that they affirm, whether that has to do with doctrine or morality or with the social, physical, or life sciences."[7] ("Autograph" in this context means the original manuscript that came from the inspired author's pen or dictation, as opposed to copies made later by scribes, which may contain mistakes.)

Here is a view of inerrancy and inspiration that is not merely different in degree, but in principle different from that which I have just described. It involves a theory of

total inerrancy that, since it moves into the fields of
social, physical, and life sciences, is subject to the conditions of those disciplines. Therefore its claim is no longer
simply a matter of faith, but is in principle falsifiable—
that is to say, it could in principle be disproved, using the
ordinary disciplines of human knowledge.

My initial (but not therefore insignificant) problem
with such a theory of total inerrancy is that, applied to the
biblical text as a whole, it simply does not seem likely to be
the case. Or, to put the matter another way, if we hold that
it is the case, then we are involved in trying to defend,
rationalize, or explain away statements and assertions
that, if they occurred in any other document, we would
naturally regard as inconsistencies or inaccuracies. I have
already mentioned some of them—the apparent contradiction between Mark 2.26 and 1 Sam. 21.1-7, or the attribution to Jeremiah at Matthew 27.9 of a verse that appears
actually to be from Zechariah 11.13. I am not, of course,
suggesting that the matter involved in either of these
examples is very important, or that the overall meaning of
the passages in question or of the Scriptures as a whole
would change very much if the apparent inaccuracies
were put right. Neither am I suggesting that there is any
intention to deceive us—either on the part of the evangelists, or on the part of the Holy Spirit! I *am* suggesting,
however, that we ought not to pretend that what seems to
be in front of us does *not* seem to be in front of us, even if
it is something quite small. Such pretense is a deception
(even if only a self-deception) and a falsehood. The
Scriptures themselves, in many strands of tradition, teach
us repeatedly what deception and falsehood lead to, and
who is their father. Deception and falsehood in small
things will lead, before we know it, to deception and false-

hood in great. As C. S. Lewis used to point out, the trouble with trying to make yourself stupider than you are is that you very often succeed.

Let me make myself clear in a further matter. It is not, of course, the case that I have any *investment* in discovering errors in Scripture. Quite the contrary! I have been careful in what I wrote above to say only that the factual inerrancy of Scripture does not seem *likely* to be the case, not that it is not the case. It may indeed turn out that there are explanations for Mark 2.26 and Matthew 27.9 (and for every other apparent error or contradiction in Holy Scripture) that do indeed preserve everyone's reputation for factual accuracy. It would hardly be the first time that texts of Scripture, accused of error, turned out after all to be correct. My point is simply that for a Christian such considerations are, in the last analysis, irrelevant. We *know* that God speaks to us a unique and saving Word through the Scriptures, a Word that will not fail us or lead us astray, and that is all we need to know. The "how" of God's Word, and its relationship to the limitations of human knowledge, and thus to the human capacity to make mistakes, involve questions that we may certainly ask, if that kind of thing interests us, but they do not involve matters about which we need to be anxious. Shakespeare has a clock chime offstage in *Julius Caesar.*[8] No one, I suppose, imagines for a moment that for the bard's honor to be saved we must somehow show that there really *were* chiming clocks in ancient Rome, or that Shakespeare did not mean what we mean when he spoke of a chiming clock, or something of that nature. We simply smile, admit that even Shakespeare could occasionally nod,[9] and still recognize that *Julius Caesar* is a great play. My awareness of God's Word to me through the

Scriptures is at least as well able to survive a similar blow. The doctrines of inspiration and inerrancy do not, in my experience, render their object so feeble that it cannot take (so to speak) our best critical punch.

Those who uphold the view of total inerrancy that I am challenging sometimes put the question (as it was put to me recently), "Why would God choose to use a book that contained errors?" It is tempting to answer along the lines of Paul's response to those who question God's right to condemn human sin: "But who are you, a human being, to answer back to God?" (Romans 9.20). In this case, however, there is a more precise response that lies in the very nature of the biblical story. Throughout that story, we see God choosing again and again to use limited, fallible humanity in the service of grace. Why does God do that? We know that God calls people and cleanses them and forgives them and commissions them (as, for example, with the prophet Isaiah and with Saint Paul) so why does God not also make them infallible and incapable of error? Paul gives us the answer to that question in a passage that I have already cited more than once: "we have this treasure in earthen vessels, to show that the transcendent power belongs to God, and not to us" (2 Cor. 4.7). The principle here stated is, in essence, a principle that is manifest throughout the entire rule of faith, and is, indeed, the principle of the incarnation itself, wherein God "made him to be sin who knew no sin, that in him we might become the righteousness of God" (2 Cor. 5.21). To desire a "perfect" Bible is to be like those who desire a "perfect" Church. It is to show ourselves finally unwilling to accept that God's perfection of love expresses itself *precisely* through God's identification with our weakness and fallibility. As Reginald H. Fuller (a leading Anglican bibli-

cal scholar) points out, the entire salvation history is
marked by this characteristic. "All the way through, with
the Bible as with all other means God uses for our salvation, the same principle is at work: God in his wondrous
condescension stoops to use human and earthly means to
accomplish his saving purpose."[10] In view of all this, it is
perhaps not surprising that many theologians see in the
demand for a totally inerrant Bible something closely
related to the docetic heresy—the heresy of those so fascinated by what they understand to be the divinity of Christ
that they cannot accept its being bound to his humanity.

All this, of course, involves the notion of God's "condescension" (condescensio Dei) to which I referred earlier.
It is sometimes pointed out that this notion was not used
by biblical scholars in the first centuries of the Christian
era with regard to matters of factual or scientific inaccu-
racy, but only with regard to matters of language and
form.[11] This is true. The historical—and literary—critical questions that cause problems for the kind of "total
inerrancy" we are now discussing are in general
(although not altogether[12]) post-enlightenment questions. Naturally, therefore, they are not questions that
were much asked by the early scholars. But those scholars
did have critical questions of their own, notably with reference to matters of style and rhetoric, about which they
were very sensitive. They were not afraid to ask those
questions, nor were they afraid to admit when the conclusions to which they came seemed, from their point of
view, to be somewhat negative. Thus they did not pretend
that the New Testament writings always met their criteria
as to what was best in grammar or style. On the contrary,
they freely admitted the "errors" with which they were
confronted in these respects, and in making these admis-

sions they marveled at a God who could nevertheless make use of such limited vessels. It is therefore precisely in faithfulness to those early scholars that we in turn direct our critical questions to the texts, admit the errors and the human limitations with which the answers to those questions seem occasionally to confront us, and marvel, as they did, at God's willingness to use our weakness for the divine glory.

One final point must be made. It will be noted that in the passage I cited above, it is not actually claimed that the written Word of God is free from error in the manuscripts that we have of it, still less in any particular edition or translation, but only "in its original autographs." Harold Lindsell, in a still influential book published in 1976, had made exactly the same point: "The Bible in all of its parts constitutes the written Word of God to man. This Word is free from all error in its original autographs."[13] And of course, as everyone is aware, we do not have these autographs.

The advantage of this particular approach is that at a stroke it renders irrelevant most of the arguments against total inerrancy outlined in the last few pages, since they are manifestly arguments based on the biblical texts and manuscripts as we now have them, not on the autographs. It presents us, in fact, with a version of the total inerrancy theory that is in principle unassailable, since obviously one cannot disprove (or, of course, prove) *any* assertion about a collection of documents that does not exist.

The problem with this approach is, unfortunately, equally obvious. It is no longer a theory about Bibles that anyone, including its proponents, actually possesses. The Bibles in the inerrantist's hands, since they are the work of copyists, are presumably as prone to error as I think mine is. Perhaps Lindsell himself was not entirely comfortable with the position thus reached, for he offered a further observation: "the textual problems are minimal,"[14] and went on to quote F. F. Bruce: "The variant readings about which any doubt remains… affect no material question of historic fact or of Christian faith and practice."[15] I entirely agree with F. F. Bruce—and so, I suspect, would most informed Christian opinion, Anglican, Protestant, or Roman Catholic. Lindsell, however, did not seem to think that he had conceded anything, for he continued, "Therefore the variant readings offer no embarrassment to inerrancy advocates." But a few pages earlier he had asserted, "If the Scripture is inspired at all it must be infallible. *If any part of it is not infallible, then that part cannot be inspired. If inspiration allows for the possibility of error then inspiration ceases to be inspiration*" (my italics).[16] With all respect, it must be pointed out that the "possibility of error" in the Bibles that are in our hands—not serious error, not error that need worry us or affect any significant part of our faith, but error, nonetheless—is exactly what Bruce's "doubt" *does* allow. Everything else, including my problem with theories of total inerrancy, follows from that.

Notes

1. Brooke Foss Westcott, *The Bible in the Church: A Popular Account of the Collection and Reception of the Holy Scriptures in the Christian Churches*. New Edition. (London: Macmillan, 1875), x. Westcott was in as good a position as anyone to be aware of the "natural laws" that went into the formation of the Scriptures. The research into their textual transmission carried out by him and his colleague F. J. Hort laid much of the basis for our modern understanding of that process and its results.

2. Jenson, *Systematic Theology* 2.276.

3. Clement VI, *To the Catholicon of the Armenians*, 29 September, 1351.

4. *Dogmatic Constitution on Divine Revelation (Verbum Dei)* 3.11 (November 18, 1965).

5. Cited by Alois Grillmeier, *The Divine Inspiration and the Interpretation of Sacred Scripture in Commentary on the Documents of Vatican II*, Vol. 3, 205).

6. *Book of Common Prayer* (1979), 84, 119; also 47, 64-65.

7. Paul Feinberg, "The Meaning of Inerrancy," in *Inerrancy*, Norman L. Geisler, ed. (Grand Rapids, Michigan: Zondervan, 1979), 294; cited with approval in Kevin Vanhoozer, "Semantics of Biblical Literature" 103.

8. Shakespeare, *Julius Caesar* II.1.191.

9. Or was he, I sometimes wonder, having a little joke? Chiming clocks were, after all, on the cutting edge of Elizabethan technology. Did Shakespeare really not know what he was doing when he put one into ancient Rome?

10. Reginald H. Fuller, "Authority and Method: Scripture," in *The Study of Anglicanism*, Stephen Sykes and John Booty, eds., (London: SPCK / Philadelphia: Fortress, 1998), 80.

11. So D. A. Carson, "Developments in the Doctrine of Scripture" in *Hermeneutics, Authority, and Canon*, D. A. Carson and John D. Woodbridge, ed. (Carlisle: Paternoster Press, 1995), 27.

12. See below, Note 4, "On Preferring the More Difficult Reading."

13. Lindsell, *Battle for the Bible* 30-31.

14. Lindsell, *Battle for the Bible* 37.

15. Ibid.

16. Lindsell, *Battle for the Bible* 31.

CHAPTER EIGHT

The Bible as Canon

In the course of these reflections on biblical authority I have already referred several times in passing to the church's "canon" ("rule" or "standard") of scripture, and to the various ways in which the collection of books that we call the Bible was put together. Having just considered the question of biblical inspiration, this may be a good moment to turn directly to the story of the canon, since "canon" and "inspiration" are often linked in people's minds. It is true, of course, that they *are* linked, inasmuch as we believe that the books of the canon are inspired. It remains, nonetheless, that whereas inspiration and the related notion of inerrancy are most helpfully considered as matters of *faith*, the evolution of the canon involves us in what are largely questions of *history*. The story is complicated, but quite interesting. It is, I think, especially interesting to Anglicans, since the Anglican view of the canon is in some respects unique. But let us come to that in its proper place!

One fruit of post-enlightenment thinking is that we now recognize that what texts mean is not confined to what their authors intended at the time of writing. Rather, as with any personal revelation, what texts mean involves those who read and hear as well as those who write, and has elements both social and communal. So, as we have seen, we best understand scriptural inspiration as a matter of God's self-disclosure through the entire process of the creation and reception of the scriptures, down to and including the latest person who hears or reads them and seeks to respond in obedience and faith. We no longer imagine there was a particular moment in the history of the church when it was suddenly possible for some inspired person or group to say, "These are the books of the Bible!" and make a list. Rather, the recognition of canonical texts in the church was a communal process that took centuries. Indeed, unless we confine our sense of the word "church" to a single Christian denomination or group of denominations, we must confess that this process of recognition, though broadly complete, still leaves some details in need of final settlement.

As we have already noticed, the process of recognizing the canonical texts was from its beginning broadly bound up with the church's life—in particular, with her awareness that certain texts truly reflected her faith. The difference between writings that the church deemed "true and genuine and acknowledged" and others that "the heretics put forward" was, according to Eusebius in his *Ecclesiastical History,* not just that the style of the rejected books was "un-apostolic" but that the contents themselves were far from orthodox.[1]

Which books, then, are included in the Bible? Anglicans, Eastern and Russian Orthodox, mainline Protestants, and Roman Catholics recognize slightly differing canons of Holy Scripture, but all include at least the following: twenty-four books written before the birth of Jesus Christ and therefore generally referred to by Christians as "the Old Testament," mostly in Hebrew but with a few sections in Aramaic; and twenty-seven books written after the birth Christ and therefore called "the New Testament," in Greek.

That the books of the Old Testament are canonical is foundational to Christian faith. The people of God were living by these books long before they were living by the gospel, and these books gave them the terms and witness by which they apprehended the gospel. This is what Paul means when he says that Christ's death and resurrection were "in accordance with the scriptures" and when he declares that Christ is "the end" (in Paul's Greek, *telos,* the "goal" or "fulfillment") "of the law" (1 Corinthians 15.3–5, Romans 10.4). Thus it is not even the case (as people sometimes claim) that the church "appropriated" the Jewish scriptures or "adapted" them. The church, on the contrary, was *formed* in the Jewish scriptures, and from the beginning knew no way to speak of Jesus Christ or the gospel except in terms of those scriptures, as he himself spoke, declaring, according to Luke, "Today this scripture has been fulfilled in your hearing" (Luke 4.21). In one way, the gospel might be said to stand or fall by that claim. Therefore, the only proper question to ask was not the one that Marcion asked and answered in the negative—"Does the Old Testament fit the gospel?"—but rather the question that Paul asked: "Do we then overthrow the law [implying, of course, the whole scriptural tradition] by this faith?" Paul's answer was unequivocal, "By no means! On the contrary, we uphold the law" (Romans 3.31). If that were not true, then, as Paul saw, the faithfulness and justice of God were called into question, and the gospel itself had no basis.

The question of precisely which books constitute the Old Testament is complicated by the fact that at the beginning of the Christian era the canon of Jewish scripture was still fluid. The exact process, criteria, and timeframe by which the Jewish canon was eventually defined are uncertain. It is clear, however, that by the end of the second Christian century the rabbis had excluded from their scriptures the additional Old Testament books that we now call "apocryphal" or "deuterocanonical." It is equally clear that these books continued to be used by Christians, who had already come to regard them as holy. In other words, though the church inherited scriptures from Judaism, it did not inherit a *canon* of scripture. The church determined its canon for itself.

Nevertheless, once the Jewish canon had been established, it did exercise an influence on the Christian, especially in the East. Hence such Christian authorities in antiquity as Athanasius of Alexandria, Hilary of Poitiers, Gregory of Nazianzus, and Jerome all claimed in one way or another that a distinction must be made between the books that comprised the Jewish canon and the others, and expressed varying degrees of reservation about the latter. The immensely prestigious Jerome was, apparently, the first to call them "apocrypha" (that is, "secret," or "of unknown origin"),[2] and he said of them also that they were to be read "for the edification of the people, but not to confirm the authority of church doctrines."[3]

Following the Reformation, Protestant tradition also referred to books not found in the Jewish canon as "apocryphal" and excluded them from the canon, while Roman Catholic scholars called them "deuterocanonical" (indicating that they were added later to the canon, in distinction from "protocanonical" books of which there was never any doubt) but continued to treat them as part of the canon, excluding only 1 and 2 Esdras and the Prayer of Manasses.

Anglicans, however, had their own solution. In the Articles of Religion, Article VI noted that "in the name of Holy Scripture we do understand those canonical Books of the Old and New Testament, of whose authority was never any doubt in the Church."[4] The article then listed not only the books found in the Jewish canon, but also "the other Books," citing Jerome to the effect that the church reads these latter "for example of life and instruction of manners; but yet doth it not apply them to establish any doctrine." These "other" books are 1 and 2 Esdras (referred to, however, as "third" and "fourth"—their titles in the Latin Vulgate), Tobit (referred to as "Tobias"), Judith, the rest of the book of Esther, Wisdom, Sirach, Baruch, The Song of the Three Children, Susanna, Bel and the Dragon, the Prayer of Manasses, and 1 and 2 Maccabees. In short, Anglicans shared antiquity's reservations over the deuterocanonical books, yet, in contrast to the Protestant churches, remained committed to retaining them within the general category of Holy Scripture, and thus both sacred and canonical.

There were important reasons for this decision. It is theologically important for Jews that the scriptures end with 2 Chronicles—and, more precisely, with the words of Cyrus the King:

> The LORD, the God of heaven, has given me all the kingdoms of the earth, and he has charged me to build him a house at Jerusalem, which is in Judah. Whoever is

among you of all his people, may the LORD his God be
with him! Let him go up! (2 Chronicles 36.23)

In other words, the Jewish scriptures end with the exhortation to and promise of *aliyah* ("going up") to the land
of Israel. That is how Jews tell the story that defines their
understanding of God's dealing with them; and that,
therefore, is how the books of scripture are arranged in
Jewish Bibles.

For Christians, by contrast, who see that story continuing with the coming of Jesus the Messiah, it is important
that the books be arranged so that Malachi stand last,
with its promise and its warning:

> Lo, I will send you the prophet Elijah before the great
> and terrible day of the LORD comes. He will turn the
> hearts of parents to their children and the hearts of chil-
> dren to their parents, so that I will not come and strike
> the land with a curse. (Malachi 4.5–6)

That is how we tell the story that defines our understanding of God's dealing with us. In narrating what we
regard as the essential "salvation history" before the coming of Jesus, no doubt these books, thus rearranged for
the purposes of our Christian Old Testament, are
enough.

The particular view of the Anglican reformers
reminds us, however, that while this is true, it is also
important that we do not simply *ignore* what happened
between Malachi and the coming of Jesus. If we do ignore
it, then we (so to speak) fall asleep one evening in a largely Semitic and Persian world, and wake up on what
appears to be the following morning in a Greco-Roman
world. We fall asleep in one kind of Israel, and wake up in
another that faces us with innumerable puzzles. It is not

surprising that we should be confused, because it is as if we had been like Rumpelstiltskin, asleep for four hundred years! Much happened to God's people in that four hundred years, and the apocryphal books tell us something of what it was. That is why we need them. We read them, as the framers of Article VI pointed out, because they provide us with "examples of life" that spring from a part of our story, our memory—not, of course, so important a part as Creation and Fall, the call of Abraham, the giving of the Law, or the sending into exile (as the framers of the article noted, we do not use them "to establish any doctrine"), but a part of our story nonetheless, and therefore not to be ignored or forgotten.

The New Testament

We have already noted that there is a close and continuing relationship between the formation of the canon and the church's rule of faith. Within this scheme, it is the particular role of the New Testament to witness to the death and, above all, the resurrection of Jesus Christ. Obviously there are also *differences* among various New Testament theologies, but their witness to God who raised Jesus from the dead is the essential thing that binds the collection together. Anyone who refuses to see that is simply refusing to take the New Testament seriously as a collection of texts. However "strange and admirable" that collection is in many ways, on this basic level of narrative it is actually quite straightforward. The fact that it shows us that even in apostolic times there were squabbles about what the story of God and Jesus actually meant, and how those who believed it were to live, should not surprise but comfort us. It binds the apostles to the rest of us, who have been squabbling about these matters ever since.

What the varieties of New Testament evidence do *not* do (or, at any rate, do not do when they are understood properly) is undermine the significance and centrality of the apostolic gospel itself. Perhaps with our own criteria of discernment we might have chosen somewhat different books to witness to that gospel, had we been given the task that faced the early church. Nevertheless, with the New Testament as it has come down to us, we have what we need to establish the apostolic witness that God raised Jesus from the dead, and that, basically, is all we need. The task does not need to be done again.

So we must recognize the utter irrelevance of questions such as, "What if we found another epistle of St. Paul?" What if we did? We should treasure it, no doubt. But it would make no difference to the apostolic gospel, and so its inclusion in the New Testament would be a matter of complete indifference. The alternative is to suppose that a new Pauline letter *would* in some way alter the apostolic gospel. In that case, the church has not understood that gospel from the second generation onward, and in *that* case, we have no criteria by which to judge what the gospel was, or should have been, anyway. We will, once again, have sawn off the branch on which we were sitting.

Article VI of the Church of England concluded that "all the Books of the New Testament, as they are commonly received, we do receive, and account them Canonical." The article had already observed that these books were those "of whose authority was never any doubt in the Church." Just as critical scholarship correctly points to differences of approach within the books of the New Testament, so it also obliges us to concede that historically the matter of their selection and recognition was not quite so simple as the article suggests. Various theologians of the church at various times in antiquity did express uncertainties about the Revelation to John (the Apocalypse), Hebrews, James, 2 and 3 John, 2 Peter, and Jude. Such doubts continued to be voiced as late as the Reformation. Martin Luther said of the Apocalypse in his 1522 Preface, "I can in no way detect that the Holy Spirit produced it.... Christ is neither taught nor known in it." He relegated it, together with Hebrews and the letter of James, to the appendix of his Bible. Although in 1545 Luther reversed his opinion, his first thoughts on the subject remain powerful. Thomas Cranmer made no statements about the canonicity of the Apocalypse, but it is notable that (in contrast to his quite extensive use of the Apocrypha) he did not include any readings from it in the daily office lectionary of his prayer book.

Despite this, it may reasonably be claimed that Christians did move quite rapidly to a consensus on the New Testament and have broadly held to it. Origen (born 185) and Eusebius of Caesarea (born 270) both give accounts of the New Testament books that, though in some respects confusing, are at least clear enough for us to say that the list of books they regarded as canonical was more or less the same as ours. Athanasius in his *Festal Letter* of 367 gave a list exactly corresponding with ours, as did the Synod of Hippo Regius in 393, at which Augustine was present. On the question of the New Testament, then, Article VI may fairly be said to have reflected the common tradition of the church.

I have said that faithful biblical study must be consciously ecumenical, and I hope that the denominational differences explored in this chapter will not be seen as a departure from that. I have taken some care to explain the particularly Anglican view of the canon because it appears to be less well known (even among Anglicans) than it ought to be, and also because it is interesting in itself. Given our overall agreement on the mass of scripture, it does not appear to me that the different views that Roman Catholics, Protestants, and Anglicans hold of the deuterocanonical books should be an impediment to their good relationships or their overall unity in faith. In modern ecumenical study Bibles, such as *The New Oxford Annotated Bible*, interdenominational groups of scholars have arrived at ways of dealing with the apocryphal books that allow all to be faithful to their own traditions and insights. Furthermore, most interdenominational ecumenical discussions (such as the ARCIC conversations between Roman Catholics and Anglicans) do not seem to have considered the issue even significant enough to be raised.

As for the specifically Anglican position, it should be noted that, even in an age of polemic, Article VI was hardly that. It cited Jerome, but in contrast to Jerome its form was notably neither prescriptive, admonitory, nor exhortatory, but descriptive. The apocryphal books, it observed, *are* in fact read for the improvement of morals and manners, and the church does *not* in fact use them to "establish any doctrine." It would be hard to see how that statement could be denied even among those denominations and groups most adamant in their claims for the identical authority of protocanonical and deuterocanonical books. For what single significant article of faith would anyone claim was *established* on the testimony of the latter? Thus, for example, we treasure Wisdom's testimony to God's love and faithfulness toward the faithful departed: "The souls of the righteous are in the hand of

God.... Their hope is full of immortality" (Wisdom 3.1, 4). But we have other texts by which we establish that hope, such as those of Paul, "For as all die in Adam, so all will be made alive in Christ" (1 Corinthians 15.22). Without the testimony of Wisdom, our liturgy and our prayers would be impoverished, but our faith would not be changed.[5]

Notes

1. Eusebius, *Ecclesiastical History.*

2. *Prologus Sancti Hieronymi in Libro Regum* 54 in *Biblia Sacra Iuxta Vulgatam Versionem* (Stuttgart: Deutsche Bibelgesellschaft, 1969), 365.

3. *Prologus Hieronymi in Libris Salomonis* 19-21 in *Biblia Sacra* 957.

4. Articles of Religion in *BCP* 1979, 868-69.

5. From time to time I am asked about the church's attitude to certain other books of a sacred character, such as the *Shepherd of Hermas* and the so-called *Gospel of Thomas*—the latter having gained a certain notoriety as a result of its frequent citation by the Jesus Seminar. From the viewpoint of the present discussion, it is perhaps enough to note that such books did indeed linger for a while in antiquity on the edge of the New Testament, and in some cases were accepted for a period by some individuals and some groups. Such apocryphal and pseudepigraphical ("falsely attributed") books are of interest to us as illustrating ideas and aspirations of the ages that produced them. It remains, nevertheless, that these books have never been recognized as canonical by any consensus of the whole church, nor even by any major Christian denomination, and probably never will be.

CHAPTER NINE

The Bíble as Authorítatíve

We believe then that our canonical scriptures are a work of divine self-revelation, a book of meeting with God, a book uniquely inspired by God. It is then not surprising that we have long claimed for the Scriptures *auctoritas*, "authority." But just what do we mean by that? "Authority," as I pointed out in the prologue to these notes, is not a very clear idea. The *Oxford English Dictionary* presents us with a whole range of meanings that have been attached to the word in the course of ordinary English usage.

Still we can, I think, say something useful about the type of thing we are (or ought to be) talking about when we speak of biblical "authority." Although the notion of "authority" is confusing, and the word can have a range of meanings, still it is possible to distinguish with at least reasonable clarity between two extremes, represented in two main senses distinguished by the *Oxford English Dictionary*. On the one hand we have, "power to enforce obedience," and on the other, "power to influence action, opinion, or belief."[1]

The former type of authority we may conveniently characterize as "coercive," since it is, in the last analysis, unilateral and unconditional. In its most extreme form ("I've got a gun and if you don't do what I want I'll blow your head off!") it is the authority of the bank robber, the terrorist, and the tyrant. The second type of authority I will characterize by the generally obsolete adjective "appellatory,"[2] since it has essentially the nature of an appeal. This, in its most extreme form, is the kind of authority that resides in the claim made on me by beauty, justice, or love. It is the kind of authority that lies in the appeal of a lover, a friend, or a faithful servant. It is the authority exercised by Beatrice in Shakespeare's *Much Ado About Nothing,* when she persuades Benedict to fight for the honor of their grievously wronged friend.[3] It is the authority exercised by Nathan the prophet when he rebukes his master King David for the murder of Uriah the Hittite (2 Samuel 12.11–15).

At first sight, appellatory authority seems much weaker than coercive. What, after all, can be done to us if we deny or destroy beauty, whose argument is, as Shakespeare observed, "no stronger than a flower"? What could Beatrice have done to Benedict if he had refused? What could Nathan have done to King David? At a deeper level, however, appellatory authority actually turns out to be the stronger of the two. Why? Because to turn from it invariably diminishes *me.* The authority of the terrorist is fierce and frightening—but if I can somehow give him the slip and get away from him without getting my head blown off, no one will blame me for it, and I will probably think myself pretty clever, and even something of a hero, for outwitting a thug. If, on the other hand, I deny justice, love, or beauty, if I refuse the appeal or rebuke of a faithful friend, then I know in my heart that somehow I have become less then I was, or might have been. I have already referred to C. S. Lewis's dictum that if we insist on pretending to be more stupid than we are, we end up becoming as stupid as we are pretending to be. It is the same, I suspect, with pretending to be less sensitive, less loving, or less appreciative, than we really are.

The converse is also true. A terrorist or a tyrant may kill me for standing in his way, but no one except a fool thinks that he has thereby demeaned me. In Shakespeare's *Richard III,* Buckingham dies, in effect, for refusing to agree to the murder of the little princes in the Tower. Far from seeing him demeaned by this, we consider that it is the first time in the play that he has acted with anything like humanity. Richard, by contrast, merely appears even more to be what he has been becoming all the time, a monster.

Now if the observations in this book have so far pointed anywhere, it is surely to suggest that the engagement God offers to us in the Bible is essentially of the appellatory kind, rather than the coercive. All that we have said of the Bible as a book of meeting, of the risk that God takes in that self-revelation, and in the human freedom to respond or not respond that is implied by that revelation—all surely point in the same direction. It is, moreover, striking that the evangelists consistently show Jesus himself distinguishing coercive authority from appellatory, and declaring the latter to be normative for all who claim authority his name:

> You know that among the Gentiles those whom they
> recognize as their rulers lord it over them, and their

great ones are tyrants over them. But it is not so among you; but whoever wishes to become great among you must be your servant, and whoever wishes to be first among you must be slave of all. For the Son of Man came not to be served but to serve, and to give his life a ransom for many. (Mark 10.42–45)

Hence the inseparable link between *suffering* and authority in the Christian community, and the gross misunderstanding displayed by those who dispute about who is to be greatest in that community. In this spirit, and perhaps with these or similar expressions in mind, the writer of 1 Peter also describes the apostolic model of authority:

Tend the flock of God that is your charge, exercising the oversight, not under compulsion but willingly, as God would have you do it—not for sordid gain but eagerly. Do not lord it over those in your charge, but be examples to the flock. And when the chief shepherd appears, you will win the crown of glory that never fades away. (1 Peter 5.2–4)

The authority of God as presented in the Bible is invariably appellatory, as Saint Paul saw—so in his letter to the Romans, he quoted Isaiah 65.2: "All day long I have held out my hands to a disobedient and contrary people" (Romans 10.21). God, from the Fall onward, is always appealing to humankind—"Where are you?"—and always it is Adam who is hiding (Genesis 3.8–10). So, at every crucial moment in the biblical story—in the lives of Abraham, Isaac, Jacob, Moses, the judges, the prophets, Mary, Paul—God *calls*. All that we said earlier of the risk that God takes in addressing us is relevant here. God calls, and we are free to respond faithfully—or not.

God's relationship with us in these narratives is then essentially as the poet Francis Thompson described it in his poem *The Hound of Heaven*:[4] a patient, unswerving pursuit, until, "in Christ God was reconciling the world to himself, not counting their trespasses against them" (2 Corinthians 5.19). Notice that God was reconciling the world "to himself." It is not the case that God was reconciling himself to the world. In the biblical view, it is the world that does not wish to be friendly with God, not God who does not wish to be friendly with the world. Damnation is a human choice, not God's: "And this is the judgment, that the light has come into the world, and people loved darkness rather than light because their deeds were evil" (John 3.19).

So, if the scriptures are properly called God's Word and if they reflect divine authority, this will be the type of their authority, too. Scriptural authority is *not* to be found in clear-cut, unarguable propositions, prohibitions, or descriptions, as if the Bible were a book of instructions for getting the universe to function. Scriptural authority will always be in the nature of an appeal. "Come now, let us argue it out, says the LORD" (Isaiah 1.18).

It is certainly no coincidence that, as Northrop Frye pointed out, of the four modes of language that we distinguished earlier, the first three tend always to compulsion: the compulsion to accept facts, the compulsion to accept the logic of an argument, the compulsion to accept social pressure. Only the last mode, the visionary and imaginative, implies no such compulsion, and that is the mode that is characteristic of scripture. Only the visionary can be a basis for words that go beyond words to something that may be a model for life itself: a "myth to live by," a *kerygma*.[5]

We do not always find this view of scriptural authority easy to accept. We tend for much of the time to prefer, or think we prefer, coercive authority to appellatory. So Paul pointed out to the Corinthians, contrasting with bitter irony the style of authority exercised by other teachers to his own:

> For you put up with it when someone makes slaves of you, or preys upon you, or takes advantage of you, or puts on airs, or gives you a slap in the face. To my shame, I must say, we were too weak for that! (2 Corinthians 11.20–21)

The authority of scripture, like the authority of Paul and the authority of Christ, lies essentially in its invitation to enter into a relationship and to share a life. The Bible, as I have said, is a place of meeting, a book of meeting; and such meeting, as I have also said, involves a risk, for God and for us.

Notes

1. *OED2*, "authority," I and II.
2. *OED2*, "appellatory."
3. Shakespeare, *Much Ado About Nothing* IV.1.257-end.
4. Francis Thompson, *The Hound of Heaven* (New York: Dodd, Mead and Company, 1922).
5. Northrop Frye, *Words with Power: Being a Second Study of "The Bible and Literature"* (San Diego: Harcourt, Brace, Jovanovich, 1990), 116–17.

PART II

What Should
We Do?

CHAPTER TEN

Listening to the Bible

What then should we do? What will the church look like, when it takes the authority of scripture seriously?

First, the church will attend to the voice of scripture in the same way that we attend to any voice whose concerns and opinions we take seriously: which is to say, the church will *listen* to it. The church that truly acknowledges the authority of scripture is not the church that shouts loudest about the subject or makes the loftiest declarations. It is the church that reads and listens to scripture, bathing in it and absorbing it, at the daily office and at the eucharist, in public prayer and in private, in Bible classes and study groups, lay and ordained, day by day, week by week. This can hardly be said too clearly. Of course we believe that there are other sources of divine revelation than the Bible: "the heavens declare the glory." Yet it remains that this is the text we privilege above all others, and therefore to its voice we pay special attention.[1]

The privileging of scripture in the eucharist and at the daily office points to the importance of our appointed lectionaries. Doubtless no lectionary is perfect, and those who use them will find occasions when the choices they offer seem strange or frustrating. Nonetheless, by means of our faithfulness to appointed lectionaries we go some way to assuring that, week in and week out, day in and day out, we are confronted not just by parts of the Bible that we might have chosen to hear and reflect on, but by passages that come to us from outside ourselves—perhaps by the very passages that we would *not* have chosen. Nothing could remind us more effectively that we do not create the gospel and its call, but rather the call of God in Christ creates us, shaping us and challenging us as the Spirit wills. Whatever the shape and style of our particular and private prayer life, the divine office said daily confronts us with something near to the whole of scripture: and that is one reason why all who take seriously their engagement with the life of faith do well to undertake its daily recitation. Those who are ordained are, of course, bound to that recitation by their vows of ordination.

The privileging of scripture in our worship says something important about the substance of preaching, and what we should look for in preaching, whether we preach ourselves or participate in preaching by listening. Of course no one may dictate on any particular occasion what the homily must contain. Occasions arise in every preacher's life when something must be said, and it must be said with the authority of the pulpit, come what may. That may be granted. But once it is granted, it should also be noted that that is the special occasion, even the rare occasion. Most of the time the preacher's job is either to expound some element of the rule of faith, the apostolic gospel—the seasons of Christmas, Easter, and Advent all point to such moments, and all, of course, are parts of the biblical story—or else the preacher's job is simply to expound the whole or some part of the biblical passages appointed for the day, relating it to the gospel of Jesus Christ on the one hand and to the lives of the people on the other, as best he or she may. Even at the great seasons, often the best way of talking of the mystery of Christmas or Easter is in fact to expound and interpret some part or parts of the appointed scriptures, so that the two tasks become one.

To put it another way: the task of preachers, the proper purpose of the homily, is to take the language of Zion—the language and stories of the Bible—and translate them into the language of those who listen. Of course the task is impossible. Who are we to take it upon ourselves to interpret God's word for God's people? Every preacher speaks as a fool! Nevertheless, preachers do not take this task upon themselves; rather, it is laid upon them. "Woe is me if I do not preach the gospel!" And every preacher speaks with the assurance of divine assistance: "Lo, I am with you always." So preachers are not to worry about their inadequacies, about which, as about all things, God is doubtless rather better informed than they are. They are to do what they are appointed to do as faithfully as they can.

My seminarian students come to me from time to time anxious because they cannot get an "idea" for their homily. They seem to feel that somehow they should have an original, entrancing "message from heaven," and that lacking such inspiration they have nothing to say. The solution to their problem is that as preachers they already *have* a message from heaven. It is in the appointed texts.

When in doubt, they are to *serve the texts,* or some part of the texts. This may not seem to be very exciting, but it happens to be the job. Of course, this means serious work. They have to wrestle with the texts, tease them, read commentaries on them, and pray over them. That is their work, and they should simply *do* it, whether they are in the mood for it or not and whether they feel "inspired" or not. Then they should tell the people what they think the text is saying, whether they think they have come up with anything interesting or original or not. They are to do it, just as millions of other men and women simply do their jobs. The entire experience of the saints is there to assure them that where they do the job faithfully, they may safely leave the result to God.

Just as the Bible is read and preached upon in community, so it should be studied in community. That is how the people of God have used their sacred texts from the beginning. Notice how often Paul's letters begin with a joint attribution of authorship, such as "Paul...and Sosthenes our brother," or "Paul...and Timothy our brother" to "the church of God" at such and such a place. I do not for one moment think that those attributions were mere convention or politeness on Paul's part. They reflected his awareness that the theological insights of the letter, the interpretations of scripture that it contained, and above all, the guidance of the Spirit that created it, had come to Paul and his friends and students together. They had clustered together to form a "house of interpretation" (Hebrew, *beit ha-midrash*). They had worked and wrestled and argued together through the meaning of the sacred texts. In particular, they had struggled to discern what those texts might mean for themselves and for the churches that Paul addressed. So when we form our Bible study groups, when we in our turn argue and struggle together over the meaning of our texts, we join a tradition that is as old (and indeed older) than Christianity itself.

There are, said Rudyard Kipling in one of his more whimsical moments,

Five and twenty ways
Of constructing tribal lays,
And every single one of them is right.

There are probably as many ways of running Bible study groups, all the way from scholarly encounter, using the best resources of commentary and lexicon available, to an almost purely meditational approach with long periods of silent and prayerful reflection. All have their place. But whatever style of Bible study we choose, unless we have decided simply to work through a particular book of the Bible (which can be a very useful exercise), the lectionary may play a part. Many of us find our Sunday worship enriched and our hearts stirred by having shared with a group of friends during the previous week an hour or so's reflection on the gospel for the coming Sunday. In another year, perhaps we may take the Old Testament reading, or the portion appointed for the epistle. There are many possibilities and the joy is, as Kipling said, that every single one of them is right.

One caution may be offered, however, even at this point. We may argue over our texts as much as we will. Christians have never been afraid of argument. But there are conditions. Whatever our disagreements, we argue together as those who are members of the same household, sisters and brothers in Christ, bound to the same rule of faith. What that means for practical purposes is

that, whatever our disagreements, we will always be willing to end together in prayer, bowing our heads together
before the One who knows all things, including the secrets
of our hearts, and of whose majesty the wisest and clever-
est of us has but the faintest glimpse. Our arguments must
not divide us. This a subject to which I intend to return.

I have already referred to our forebears' notion of *perspicuitas*, or "clarity"—that where the scriptures are faithfully studied, that study will bring good fruit. This is a
moment to speak more precisely of that fruit. The result
of our recitation of scripture in the office, our exposition
of scripture in preaching, and our study of the scriptures
together will be that we are deepened in our knowledge
and understanding of the apostolic gospel, which is to
say, our knowledge and understanding of Jesus Christ.
Wherever that is done, there the church is edified (that is,
"built up") and sanctified (that is, "made holy," "set
apart," "consecrated" as God's own).

Are there any guidelines as to how we might expect
this to happen? Are there particular questions that we
might put to the scriptures and expect them to answer
them? I believe there are, and that the church's own traditions of biblical interpretation can give us useful point-
ers. Earlier in this book I mentioned the "four senses" of
scripture for which Christian scholars customarily
looked in the Middle Ages. Augustine of Dacia, an
Augustinian monk living in the second part of the thirteenth century, summed up these four senses in four lines
of execrably bad Latin verse that may, however, be translated into four lines of quite reasonable English prose as
follows:

The literal sense teaches what happened,
The allegorical what you should believe,

The moral what you should do,
The anagogical what you should aim for.

In the language of our own times, we might say that we
first look to the Scriptures to see, so far as we can, what
they may have meant for those who first heard them.
This is what Augustine and those around him called the
"literal" sense. Further reflection can lead, however, to
our apprehending other implications in the texts, which
can be categorized under three heads or "senses."

First, what bearing do these texts have on our faith
now? What do they imply for faith in the twenty-first
century? This is what Augustine called their "allegorical"
sense. (Obviously, he was using the word "allegory" in its
wider—and foundational—sense of "speaking otherwise
than one seems to speak," i.e. implying without saying
directly, rather than in its narrower and now virtually
exclusive sense of describing a subject "under the guise of
some other subject.")[2]

Second, what do we learn from these texts about how
we should be acting? How should these texts affect our
behavior? This is what Augustine would have called their
"moral" sense.

And third, where then do we believe that our lives are
leading? For what do we hope? What is the "eschatological" message of the texts? This is what Augustine called
their "anagogical" sense (from a Greek word, anagō, that
meant "to lead upward").

By way of example, we might consider the New
Testament's "Slaves, obey your masters" passages to which
we have already referred more than once. Taken at the literal or historical level, these passages remind us of the
facts of the story: that slavery was a day-to-day reality of
the world in which the Bible came into being and the

gospel was first preached. Many of those who first believed were in fact slaves; others (like Philemon) were slave owners.

Further reflection on these passages may, however, lead us to gain from them other insights.

We may consider how through them we can come to understand more deeply the suffering of Christ, who also suffered as a slave for the sake of others. We may even come to understand our own sufferings as something to be endured in union with the sufferings of Christ, as some of those slaves did, and as Paul seems to have understood his suffering. This would be their "allegorical" sense.

Or we may determine in an unjust situation to act with what faithfulness and grace is possible for us, as Christ did, and as the slaves were called to do. This would be their "moral" sense. Or we may reflect on our end, noting that we live in hope, as they did, knowing that we have indeed a true "master" who will finally deliver us from all oppression. This would be their "anagogical" sense.

(As one who is *not* suffering, I write these things with some trepidation, yet also with the confidence of knowing that oppressed Christians over the centuries have found these texts to be sources of encouragement, faith, and hope in precisely this way.)

This kind of exegesis seeks to relate the texts of the Bible to Christ and the apostolic gospel. More precisely, the allegorical sense points us to the Christ who came to us, and so to a deeper understanding of the incarnation; the moral sense points us to the Christ who comes to us now, and who wills to enter into our hearts; and the anagogical sense points to the Christ who will come to us at the consummation. This centering upon Christ is an

important principle that must always guide such reflections. Otherwise we run the risk that our allegorical
exposition will degenerate into "what-this-passage-
means-to-me," our moral exposition into mere moraliz-
ing, and our anagogical exposition either into mere mys-
ticism or into unbridled speculation and fantasy about
the unknown future. These were not dangers that the
medieval expositors entirely avoided, and their failures in
this matter rightly led to reformation caution over the
whole approach.

Does such Christ-centered exegesis run the risk of
"spiritualizing" the text, especially with regard to the Old
Testament? Of course it does, which is one reason why
exposition of the four senses must always *begin* with the
literal sense, with the best attempt we can manage to discern what the texts *actually meant* for those who composed them and first heard them, and what the events
actually were to which they referred. "I would not," wrote
Martin Luther, "have a theologian give himself to allego-
rizing until he has perfected the grammatical and literal
interpretation of the Scriptures; otherwise his theology
will bring him into danger, as Origen discovered."[3] If we
avoid the literal sense, then essentially we have avoided
the text. (I intend to say more of the discipline involved
in this, and the need for it, in my next chapter.) On the
other hand, Christian exegesis is not *merely* scientific and
historical. It is also exegesis on the basis of faith. If we
rightly call both the Old and New Testaments "the Word
of God," the place of divine self-revelation, and our book
of meeting, and if the New Testament speaks rightly of
Christ as the fulfillment of the Old, then we are *bound*
also to seek to discern the lineaments of Christ in the
Old—Christ calling us to faith and obedience, Christ

coming to us in judgment and glory. This is not a matter of "spiritualizing" the text but rather of listening to it for what we claim it says, as indeed we claim that the same thing is said by the whole universe if we have ears to hear it, for "the heavens declare the glory of God."

As to how this may work in practice as regards the Old Testament, let me offer a mild parallel from the study of other ancient literature. Many ancient texts, such as the Old English poem *Beowulf,* when they describe personal combat speak of blood "spurting" when people are wounded. But Sir William Harvey did not expound his theory of the circulation of the blood (which explains just *why* blood may spurt when someone is stabbed) until the year 1616. What then? Are the ancient writers talking about the circulation of the blood, or not? If by that question we mean, "Did the author of *Beowulf* know about Harvey's theories?", the answer is obviously, "No." If we mean, "Was he describing correctly a phenomenon of which Harvey's theories would provide us with a much fuller understanding?" the answer is, "Yes." I think the matter is somewhat parallel with our exposition of the Old Testament. The writer of Genesis tells how God spoke, and the world was created. Was the writer speaking of "the Word" that became incarnate in Jesus of Nazareth? If we mean by that question, "Did he know about the incarnation and the coming of Jesus?" the answer is, "No." If we mean, "Was he inspired to say something about the nature of the world that was true, and that we understand much more deeply *in the light of the coming of Christ?*" the answer is, "Yes, he did!" And in this case it is very easy for us to say that, because the Fourth Evangelist, the writer to the Hebrews, and the author of the christological hymn in Colossians have

already made all the essential connections for us (see
John 1.1–14, Hebrews 1.1–4, and Colossians 1.15–20). In
short, then, it is as reasonable and proper for a Christian
exegete to discern the lineaments of Christ in the Genesis
narrative as it is for a modern reader to recognize the circulation of the blood being described, albeit unknowing-
ly, in *Beowulf*'s accounts of physical wounding.

In doing this, do we then reshape and reinterpret our
tradition, and particularly Old Testament tradition? Of
course we do! But that is part of what it means to live.
Subsequent experience and subsequent reflection always
reshape and reinterpret every memory. "Now I understand!" we say of something that happened to us in the
past. The fulfillment of a promise always puts us in a new
relationship to that promise and conditions our understanding of it. My knowledge of the meaning of my mar-
riage now is not the knowledge that I had at the time of
my wedding: in some ways it is sweeter, in some ways
more bitter, in some ways richer, but it is *different* and it
is *deeper*. And so it is with communities and generations.
Paul's theology was not Isaiah's and Nicaea's theology was
not Paul's and our theology is not theirs. Part of the reason for that is that we now know more than they did, and
they are a part of what we know. That is as it should be
and must be. Such a reshaping and reinterpretation is
inherent in the Old Testament tradition itself. We can see
it in Deuteronomy (the "second law") when it reinter-
prets the first law, and in Isaiah's call to see in Israel's
redemption from the Babylonian exile a mighty act of
God that will make even the Exodus relative:

> Do not remember the former things,
>   or consider the things of old.
> I am about to do a new thing;

now it springs forth, do you not perceive it?

(Isaiah 43.18–19)

Rabbinic tradition to this day continues, in entire faithfulness to this tradition, to understand and interpret the scriptures and itself in the light of Israel's ongoing experience over the centuries.

I have gone some way from my original point, but I believe that the development and qualification of it were necessary. In sum, I am suggesting that even in the twenty-first century the four senses, suitably adapted to our age and capacities, remain an entirely balanced and sensible set of categories against which we may usefully check our own attempts to expound the Bible. I have certainly found the categories useful myself. Of course we cannot expect that all passages of scripture will move us equally at all moments with messages in all four senses. On the other hand, if we *never* see or look for more than one sense, then the chances are that our expositions lack either the preparation that comes from study (which for a Christian exegete should always be enlightened by prayer), or the engagement that comes from prayer (which for a Christian exegete should always be informed by study). And that brings me to the subject of my next chapter.

Notes

1. Nevertheless, symbolic actions are important, and I would strongly encourage treating the actual texts of scripture reverently in the course of the liturgy. I am delighted to see such reverence endorsed by current trends in the liturgical movement—by directions, for example, that the appointed minister carry the book of lections or the gospels with some ceremony in the opening and closing processions and that the minister place the book solemnly on the lectern/pulpit/ambo as its

"throne"; that for the gospel reading (the climax of the liturgy of the word) the whole assembly stands, the minister and the whole assembly cross themselves on the forehead, lips, and heart, the minister censes the book before reading the gospel and reverences the text with a kiss at the end; that the minister then elevates the book before the assembly. All these simple gestures serve to imprint in our thoughts how special these writings are. On the other hand, some very *bad* symbolism is being offered when the book is ostentatiously *removed* from its throne at sermon time in order to make way for the preacher's own notes—or else is used as a prop for them! To be fair to preachers, it has to be conceded that many lecterns are so poorly designed for their purpose there really is little option but to indulge in these unsatisfactory practices. Again, I am delighted to see liturgists encouraging us to design and adorn the (single!) lecterns in our churches in ways that will reflect the dignity of God's word and presence, just as we do with the altar.

2. OED 2, "allegory," Etymology and 1.

3. Martin Luther, *The Babylonian Captivity of the Church,* in *Works of Martin Luther,* vol. 2 (Philadelphia: United Lutheran Publication House, 1915–32), 276.

CHAPTER ELEVEN

Studying the Bible

I hear from time to time—and, indeed, I have been challenged by—those who, in the name of piety, suggest that too much intellectual and scholarly study of Bible and theology is to be avoided, for, after all, God speaks to the heart. This is a dangerous half-truth, akin to the error of preachers who interpret the divine promise that in time of persecution the Holy Spirit will put into their hearts what they ought to say as an excuse not to prepare their sermons properly. Of course God speaks to the simplest and the most unlearned, but that is no excuse for those who have gifts for serious study not to use them. That is to be like the servant who buried his talent—and without his excuse, for at least the servant was afraid. It is true that Holy Scripture portrays the Roman governor Festus crying out at Paul, "Too much learning is driving you insane!"—but it happens to be the case that Holy Scripture also makes it quite clear that Festus is wrong, for Paul responds, "I am not out of my mind, most excellent Festus, but I am speaking the sober truth" (Acts 26.24–25).

Everyone agrees, I suppose, that we study the Bible so as to understand it. But what do we mean by "understand"? Actually, we commonly use the word in two ways. We sometimes say that we have "understood" something when we mean that we have acquired and comprehended information about it: as when we understand, for example, how the internal combustion engine works. On the other hand, when Jane Austin's Emma observed that "One half of the world cannot understand the pleasures of the other," it is evident that that highly intelligent young woman was speaking not of the acquisition of knowledge, nor of apprehending of its significance, but of an attitude to what is apprehended. She was talking of a way of being, of *formation*. For me to "understand" what it is that my friend enjoys about stamp collecting would be for me to become in some sense a different person.

What then of our reading of scripture? We have described the Bible as a "book of meeting," wherein God discloses God's self to us. We have spoken of its authority as an appeal to enter into a relationship and share a life. And we have noted that relationships, unlike mere information, transform us. That, of course, is the important additional feature of our study of the Bible. We come to it looking not only for understanding in our first sense, but also for understanding in our second sense. We seek not only information, but also transformation, not merely to be told about the truth, but also to be brought into the truth.

What follows from this? If we read texts in a way that seeks only to be informed about them, we can stop there without ever considering the possibilities the texts have for transforming us. I confess I am not sure, with texts that are evidently designed to transform us, such as the

New Testament or Plato's *Republic,* that such a stopping short is ever completely defensible, even academically. The poet and mystic Charles Williams wrote a rather splendid fantasy called *The Place of the Lion,* in which a young woman named Damaris Tighe tries to study the Greek philosophers as a merely academic exercise, only to be overwhelmed when the realities with which they deal, such as justice and beauty, begin suddenly to confront her. (If you want to know what happens, you had better read the book!) I sometimes think that all who study great texts should be obliged to read *The Place of the Lion* before they start. Be that as it may, at least I grant that reading the Bible or other great texts as if it were purely an academic exercise with no relevance to our real lives *may* be possible, and I am bound to admit that many people in modern universities attempt to do it all the time.

But the converse, I am sure, is not possible. If we are concerned about the transformative possibilities of a text, we must also be concerned with being informed about it. For how can we honestly claim to have been transformed by a text, unless we have done our best to know what the text actually says? That, of course, is why, as we saw earlier, the ancients rightly insisted that the literal sense of scripture—the straightforward sense, the historical sense—must be explored first, before the other three senses could be examined. In other words, we must be prepared to engage in the ordinary, serious, left-brain work that is involved in understanding any text, and particularly any ancient text: the best textual, linguistic, historical, social, and literary study that we can manage. That is the way we can acquire the kind of knowledge that will help us understand these texts in particular, and if they are what we claim they are, we owe them that.[1]

Thus, to name a field of concern that happens to be a particular interest of mine, I am repeatedly surprised by the number of those who claim to interpret the New Testament, and even publish books about it, without ever troubling to ask themselves what kind of texts they are examining—in other words, without paying any attention to what literary critics refer to as the problem of "genre." Yet genre is a tool of meaning. If we do not know the genre of the words we are studying, the chances of our understanding them as their author intended are slim indeed. Imagine what would happen if we were to treat a joke as a serious piece of factual reporting ("But *why* did the chicken want to get to the other side?")!

Yet that is exactly what is happening when people comment adversely on Paul's "arrogance" in offering himself as a moral example to his congregations, or when interpreters of the gospels comment on Mark's inadequacies as a biographer because he never tells us anything about Jesus' psychology. This kind of criticism simply ignores the conventions that governed literature like Paul's letters and Mark's gospel. In Greco-Roman moral exhortation (of which Paul's letters are often an example) it was regarded as normal and proper to offer oneself as an example to be followed. So in his *Institutio Oratorio* the great Roman orator Quintilian wrote, "No-one will deny that the advice one gives should be in keeping with one's own manner of life."[2] In other words, if you were not prepared to practice what you advised, then you had no business offering the advice in the first place. Likewise, in Greco-Roman "lives" (of which all four of our canonical gospels are examples) it was normal for the authors to pay little or no attention to the inner motivations of their subjects, but rather to devote themselves to what the subjects said and did.

An awareness of genre is a matter of literary sensitivity. But there are, of course, many other questions to ask, such as, Are we actually reading the right text? The New Testament has come down to us through hundreds of manuscripts, and they do not all say the same thing, as anyone can see who looks at the marginal variants offered by the *Revised Standard Version*, the *New Revised Standard Version*, or the *New American Bible*. How can we decide which is the right text? *Can* we decide at all?

And what of the social conventions and assumptions that lie behind our texts? In my teaching I find it illuminating to point to five assumptions that virtually everyone who lived in the world that saw the creation of the New Testament would have shared, and that were doubtless therefore shared by the majority of those who first heard the New Testament documents read.

First, that it is impossible to be a complete human being alone. Human beings find their identity in the community of which they are part (some scholars speak of a sense of "solidarity"). Thus, modern western notions of the importance of the individual, symbolized by the "man alone" who owes nothing to others and (like heroes of some old Westerns) rides off alone into the sunset at the end of every adventure rather than be tied down to a particular place, would have seemed to them to be not so much a portrait of heroism as of damnation.

Second, that human society naturally runs on the basis of "patronage"—which means that it is the duty of the rich and powerful to be benefactors of the poor and weak, and the duty of those so benefitted to feel a proper sense of obligation to their benefactors (therefore scholars speak of the world of this period as a "patronage society").

Third, that human beings naturally live on the basis of "honor" and seek to avoid "shame"—"honor" in this context being a combination of the value you have in your own eyes together with the value you have in the eyes of whomever is important to you (therefore scholars also speak of the world of this period as an "honor-shame" society).

Fourth, that some people would inevitably find themselves, for a variety of reasons, the property of others (slavery).

And fifth, that it was in general the role of men to be in charge of things, and of women to be subordinate (patriarchy).

These five assumptions were a part of the air that everyone breathed in the first century of the Christian era, and of course they are reflected again and again throughout the New Testament. To be surprised at or critical of this—to dismiss Paul, for example, as "patriarchal"—is therefore about as reasonable as to criticize him as inefficient because he did not write his letters on a laptop. The point is, if we wish to understand those who wrote the New Testament (or, indeed, any ancient text) we need first to be aware of these assumptions, and then, at least for the moment, to try the experiment of "suspending our disbelief" in regard to them. When we do that, we often discover that words that to our western, twenty-first-century ears seem at first to be encouraging of, say, patriarchy or slavery, *when heard in the context in which they were originally uttered,* actually turn out to have been moving in a direction that undermined those institutions—and would so have appeared to their contemporaries.

By way of example, let us return yet again to our "pro-slavery" texts. There are, as we have noticed, a number of passages in both Old and New Testaments indicating that those who wrote them accepted slavery as an institution, and undoubtedly the existence of these passages was one reason why some slave owners in the seventeenth century did not mind missionaries baptizing their slaves. On the other hand, as we also noted, the slaves themselves then turned to quite different passages, such as God's words to Pharaoh, "Let my people go!" and Paul's words to the Galatians about the implications of the baptismal covenant. The point to be made now, however, is this: that in choosing the texts that they would apply to their situation, the slaves actually showed themselves to be much better interpreters of Scripture than their masters and the pro-slavery preachers. For in selecting the story of the Exodus and Paul's description of the baptismal covenant, they had chosen passages that were closely bound up with the Rule of Faith itself, and therefore with the essential and universal nature of God's relationship to God's people. The masters and the pro-slavery preachers, by contrast, were appealing to passages that were evidently *ad hoc* and *ad hominem*: that is to say, passages evidently aimed, not at stating universal norms, but rather at the particular situation that confronted the writers. For given the realities of first century society—wherein slave owners were entirely within their rights to kill their slaves if they wished to do so—it is hard to see what general advice Paul and others *could* reasonably or responsibly have given to their converts save, "obey your masters"!

Then there is the letter to Philemon, wherein Paul, while conforming to institutional norms and returning the runaway slave Onesimus to his master, notes that since Onesimus is now baptized, Philemon will be receiving back "no longer as a slave but more than a slave, a beloved brother" (15–16). Given ancient assumptions about slavery, perhaps Paul himself did not entirely see the implications of what he was saying. With hindsight, however, it is hard to see how such a view of the relationship of Christian slave and Christian master could have failed, ultimately, to undermine slavery as an institution.

All that granted, we might also come to the conclusion that some of the assumptions of the ancient world have something to teach us. As C. S. Lewis used to say, the ancients made mistakes, but at least they were not our mistakes, so there is always the possibility that we can learn from them. Particularly, I suspect, we can learn something from their understanding of community, so much at odds with our modern, western individualism.

Nevertheless, study alone will not get us where we need to go (see John 5.39!). Some, indeed, find that historical study of the Bible seems actually to cut them off from its message. Richard Hays, in a recent book on *The Moral Vision of the New Testament,* speaks of a pastor in Kansas who attended a seminar on the Bible that Hays was leading. In the course of this seminar, Hays persuaded the pastor (correctly, in my opinion) that Paul's immediate concern in the letter to the Romans was to explain the relationship of Jew and gentile in the providence of God, and to make clear that God's grace in the gospel does not abrogate God's faithfulness to Israel. The pastor responded, "Professor Hays, you've convinced me that you're right about Romans, but now I don't see how

I can preach from it any more. Where I serve out in Western Kansas, Israel's fate isn't a burning issue for my people, and there's not a Jew within a hundred miles of my church."[3]

In tandem with that—or perhaps a better metaphor would be to say, as the reverse side of the same coin—I would cite a recent critique of my own book, *A Preface to Romans*[4] (a critique that was, let me hasten to say, both thoughtful and generous). The reviewer asked me a number of questions, one of which was this: Granted that I see Romans as relevant to contemporary preachers, does not my approach risk "confining the results of [my] analysis to the interpretive concerns of another time, place, and person than the mid-first century, Cenchreae and Rome, or Paul?"[5] In other words, if we succeed in locating Paul properly in the first century, have we lost him for twentieth-century Kansas? On the other hand, if see in him elements that are relevant to twentieth-century Kansas, must we have lost him for the first century?

Both questioners point to a real problem; and both, in my view, so present the problem as to overstate it. Yes, it is true that we can no longer assume that what ancient writers say about particular questions can be applied without remainder to our own situations—we have already noted how we have to set in wider context what some biblical passages say about matters such as slavery. Yes, it is true that an imaginative leap is required to go between Paul's situation and ours. Nevertheless, the leap is scarcely impossible. The fact is, the human heart is as prone now as it was then to the arrogance and self-righteousness that made it difficult for the Roman Jews and gentiles to "welcome one another, therefore, just as Christ had welcomed [them], for the glory of God" (Romans

15.7), and that alone makes Paul's concerns in the letter to the Romans as relevant in the twenty-first century as they were in the first.

We can use the "pastness" of the past as a means of shielding ourselves from its challenges if we wish: and in that way we can excuse ourselves from admitting that anyone of another generation or culture could have anything to say to us. But if we do, we indulge in an illusion that is, I suspect, far more dangerous and absurd than the assumption that writers in the past simply wrote to people and situations that are the same as ours. This, as I observed earlier, is the point made by Charles Williams in his novel *The Place of the Lion*. Williams was, of course, essentially a poet, a novelist, and a literary critic rather than a theologian, and perhaps a dose of the experience of the great literature of the past is the best cure for this particular illusion. Millions of people in virtually every culture all over the world continue to perform, watch, and be enthralled by Shakespeare, to smile over Geoffrey Chaucer and Jane Austin, to be disturbed and fascinated by Homer and Virgil and Dante and Dostoevsky. They do not do this simply because they find the works of these authors to be interesting but ultimately incomprehensible historical exercises. Quite the contrary! Faced by Dante's

> In the middle of the journey of our life
> I came to myself by way of a dark wood
> Where the straight way was lost

we are grasped and fascinated precisely because we *do* know something of what Dante was talking about. Life at the turn of the thirteenth century was vastly different from that at the turn of the twenty-first, but not utterly different. When Dante goes on to say,

> I know not how to say well how I came there,
> so full was I of sleep at that point
> when I abandoned the right way[6]

we know, again, exactly what he is talking about. We, too, have at times found our lives to be far from where they should have been or where we wanted them to be, and yet have scarcely any recollection of the decisions that led us to that place.

So much may be said in general terms. When it comes to the matter of Christian exegesis of the scriptures, however, I would insist that the matter must be stated even more sharply. The Christian scholar studying Paul is not simply in the position of the secular academic studying Homer. Why? Because the Christian scholar studying Paul is *not,* essentially, in a different community of interpretation from Paul's. Quite the contrary! Such a scholar is still a member of the same family. *This* past is *our* past. Paul's world was different from ours and we must not forget it. Nevertheless, a sound theology will remind us that what we have in common with Paul is much more important than what divides us, for what we have in common is actually the only thing that matters, namely, that we both belong to the baptized people of God.

Hence, of course, we do not (or should not) *just* do intellectual study of the Bible—historical criticism or whatever: we also pray over it, and seek the holiness of life to which the Bible calls us. To put it another way, those who interpret scripture are attempting to do theology, and it is impossible to be a theologian without prayer and a life of attempted obedience to God.

The reasons for this, particularly in the area of appealing to and living under scriptural authority, are evident. The biblical books are, we believe, inspired by the Spirit and can only be interpreted by the Spirit. The true locus of scriptural inspiration is, I have suggested, the whole process of the Spirit's work, both in their creation and in their appropriation in and through the life of the church. Therefore, if we are not regular communicants; if we do not participate in the life of God's people; if we do not pray; if we do not try to feed the hungry and clothe the naked; if, in a word, we are not attempting to lead lives of faithful obedience, then we cannot expect to study or interpret the Bible as it was meant to be studied and interpreted, for

> "What no eye has seen, nor ear heard,
> nor the human heart conceived,
> what God has prepared for those who love him"—

> these things God has revealed to us through the Spirit; for the Spirit searches everything, even the depths of God. For what human being knows what is truly human except the human spirit that is within? So also no one comprehends what is truly God's except the Spirit of God. (1 Corinthians 2.9–11)

This means that all biblical study that can truly be called "faithful" will in some sense—formally or informally, intentionally or not—contain the elements of what has been called *lectio divina*—"sacred reading." That is to say, it will include the (comparatively) left-brain elements of reading *(lectio)* and reflection *(meditatio)*. But such "faithful" Bible study will also contain the (comparatively) right-brain activity of response *(oratio)*. This is what may arise from reflection—the sense of God's presence, thanksgiving, joy, tears, repentance, and so on. Finally, such Bible study will move in the direction of contemplation *(contemplatio)*. This is where we do our best to abandon our efforts to reflect and respond, seeking instead to rest in the mystery of God's presence and to listen, in preparation for obedience. It is in this process—the whole process—that we will come to learn what we need to learn of the four senses of scripture, and to claim them for ourselves.

This practice of prayer and quest for holiness of life is precisely what identifies us not merely as "students of religion" but as continuing members of the biblical people, as those whose story the Bible contains, and as—for all our distance from it in space and time—the community to whom its word is addressed.

Here we note, then, a further activity of the community in which biblical authority is taken seriously. In such a community we will be listening to the voice of the Bible as those who are aware that a major part of what it tells us is our own story, or, at least, the early part of that story. What we learn from the apostolic gospel, the rule of faith, is what happened *to us*. That must surely lead to a question, namely, where are we now in the story? Obviously, we are about to live out the next stage of it—a stage that will doubtless have its own characteristics, and certainly will not merely repeat what has gone before (what kind of a story would that be?), but which will presumably be consistent with earlier parts of the plot, and with characters who have appeared so far. If we wish to identify with certain characters in that story—say, its heroines and heroes—then we will need to do our best to know the story as well as we can, and to understand those characters as much as possible, opening our hearts to act consciously as they might have acted, to share in their faith, and to participate in their hope. On the other hand, we cannot possibly expect simply to look up their part of the story and read from it answers to problems confronting us. We cannot expect to do that because we are in our part of the story, not theirs. What we can do, however, is soak ourselves in their personalities, and especially in the personality of Jesus Christ.

This is exactly what Paul advises:

> Let the same mind be in you that was in Christ Jesus,
>   who, though he was in the form of God,
> did not regard equality with God
>   as something to be exploited,
>   but emptied himself,
> taking the form of a slave,
>   being born in human likeness.
> And being found in human form,
>   he humbled himself
>   and became obedient to the point of death—
> even death on a cross. (Philippians 2.5–8)

Elsewhere, Paul urges his fellow Christians to "be imitators of me, as I am of Christ" (1 Corinthians 11.1) In other words, those who seek not merely to talk but to do, not merely to claim the authority of Holy Scripture but to live under it, must first seek to be faithful to their calling as God's people. They must by all means seek to embody in themselves, so far as they are able, the imitation of Christ—the faithfulness and obedience of Jesus Christ and of his saints. Such imitation of Christ begins, if Paul's model is to be trusted, by contemplating what Christ did.

Notes

1. The *Constitution on Divine Revelation* of Vatican II (to which I have already referred in my discussion of inerrancy) puts this succinctly: "Rightly to understand what the sacred author wanted to affirm in his work, due attention must be paid both to the customary and characteristic patterns of perception, speech and narrative which prevailed at the age of the sacred writer, and to the conventions which the people of that time followed in their dealings with one another" (3.12).

2. Quintilian, *Institutio Oratorio* 3.13.

3. Richard B. Hays, *The Moral Vision of the New Testament: Community, Cross, New Creation: A Contemporary Introduction to New Testament Ethics* (San Francisco: HarperSanFransisco, 1996).

4. Christopher Bryan, *A Preface to Romans: Notes on the Epistle in Its Literary and Social Setting* (New York: Oxford University Press, 2000). As it happens, in this study I touch on the problem of historical consciousness and its effect on our relationship to the texts, contrasting it with the approach of the ancient literary critics (see pages 50–52 and literature there cited).

5. Mark D. Nanos, in *Review of Biblical Literature* at www.bookreviews.org.

6. Dante, *Commedia: Inferno* 1.1-3, 10-12.

CHAPTER TWELVE

Making Decisions in the Light of the Bible

This book began with the 1998 Lambeth Conference: with church leaders in conflict over a serious theological and moral issue and equally in conflict over how the authority of Holy Scripture might apply to that issue. Let it approach its close with an entirely *imaginary* Lambeth Conference at which the bishops have sought the present author's advice as they prepare for their deliberations. That unlikely scenario granted, let it be noted that I certainly do not think what I am about to say applies *only* to bishops. It applies to all of us, whether lay or ordained, who exercise any function involving leadership or oversight in the church at all.

First, I would point to what I have said so far. Those who are called to lead the church need to approach decision making with some informed awareness of the role that the Scriptures play, or ought to play, in that process. Those who will lead the Church need, moreover, to be sharers in the hope that the Scriptures proclaim, as well as seeking to embody the faith and obedience those Scriptures require. Those who will lead the Church are called to the imitation of Christ, and they must be willing to proclaim the apostolic gospel—the gospel of God who raised Jesus from the dead.

I confess I have little patience with those professing church leadership who do not seem to see this. Bishops, says the Ordinal of the American *Book of Common Prayer* (1979), are called to "guard the faith, unity and discipline of the Church." Therefore bishops and others in leadership roles who can no longer do that—who, for example, have "doubts" about the atoning powers of the cross, or about the resurrection, such that they cannot either keep their doubts to themselves or teach the doctrine of the cross and resurrection as the Church has taught it—such persons *ought* to resign. This is not (as some may try to make it) a matter of the church's caring or not caring for individuals, or respecting or not respecting personal rights and beliefs. I do not say that such persons must leave the church, or even that they may not participate in its life to whatever level they feel comfortable. The church can and should be welcoming to all who come to her with however vague a faith or uncertain a hope. It is not the church's job to quench smoking candles. But I am saying that for those who would *lead* the church, willingness and ability to witness to Jesus' death and resurrection are requirements and not options, and have been from the beginning of the apostolic age (see Acts 1.22). All this is a matter of common sense and common honesty, and ought to go without saying. It is one of the less pleasing aspects of the present time that apparently it needs to be said.

Next, I would suggest that those called to leadership and to participation in the decision-making processes of the church would do well, in their personal "imitation of Christ," to focus on developing two qualities in particular. The one is associated in the New Testament with behavior and decision-making in the face of disagreement. The other is associated with leadership.

The former of these qualities is *sōphrosunē*—"thinking soberly," a notion associated by the ancients with prudence, reasonableness, and moderation. It is the very first quality that Paul urges the fractured Roman church to seek in the pursuance of unity in Christ (see Romans 12.3). It apparently is the quality that will enable members of that church who are from different groups and who hold different opinions to "welcome one another...just as Christ has welcomed [them]" (Romans 15.7).

In the time of Paul, in the writings of pagan, Jewish, and Christian authors alike, "thinking soberly" was connected with restraint and modesty in relation to others. So the author of Wisdom, having said that we are taught *sōphrosunē* by the divine wisdom, then links it with justice—that is, proper behavior in relation toward other people (see Wisdom 8.7). "Thinking soberly" is also, however, associated with rationality and good sense. It is therefore the exact opposite of *mania* ("frenzy") (Mark 5.15, par. Luke 8.35; Acts 26.25). In writing to the Corinthians, Paul reminds them that his "sober concern" for the community is what corresponds to a true "ecstasy" for God, and is the only behavior that can truly be said to be based on the love of Christ who "died for all" (2 Corinthians 5.13–14). He is obviously setting this attitude in contrast to certain types of *mania*—notably, party factionalism and a taste for the flashier kinds of religious experience—that were evidently quite prominent in the Corinthian church.

The latter quality to which I would draw the attention of those called to oversight among us is *praütēs*—usually translated in our English Bibles as "meekness" or "gentleness." As Deidre J. Good has recently shown us in a fine book, those who first listened to the New Testament or to the Greek version of the Old Testament would have understood by *praütēs* something they would have recognized as the classic virtue of one worthy to rule, or a true philosopher.[1] It is, according to Plato's *Phaedo,* the quality displayed by Socrates, who showed himself in his death to be "the noblest and gentlest *(praototon)* and the bravest...of men."[2] "Do nothing in anger," Isocrates wrote to Nicocles, the young King of Cyprus, "Show yourself stern by overlooking nothing that happens, but *praos*[3] by making the punishment less than the offense."[4] According to Josephus, *praütēs* was a quality both claimed and manifested by Titus during the Jewish War: that is to say, as a Roman military commander he pursued the campaign with rigor, as was proper for a soldier, but he also displayed clemency to those among the rebels who were willing to accept it.[5]

In other words, while "meekness" and "gentleness" catch something of what the ancients understood by *praütēs,* they also miss something. For *praütēs* implies combining gentleness with a degree of tough-mindedness, with oneself as well as with others, that might well be rendered in English by something like "disciplined calmness."[6] When Paul exhorts the Corinthians on the basis of the *praütēs* of Christ (2 Corinthians 10.1); when he asks them whether they wish him to come "with a

stick, or with love in a spirit of *praütēs*" (1 Corinthians
4.21); when he tells the Galatians to correct the sinner in
their midst "in the spirit of *praütēs*" (Galatians 6.1)—in
all these cases it is evident that he is speaking *both* of gentleness *and* of a firmness that remains polite—a calm,
disciplined strength. Such strength can exercise clemency
and even rebuke with courtesy, precisely because it is the
mark of those who know who and whose they are. Thus
praütēs is, like *sōphrosunē*, the exact opposite (as Paul no
doubt intended the Corinthians in particular to realize)
of the *mania* ("frenzy") of that "fool" who can only exercise authority through violence, who "makes slaves of
you, or preys upon you, or puts on airs, or gives you a slap
in the face" (2 Corinthians 11.21).[7]

"Let the same mind be among you that was in Christ
Jesus" (Philippians 2.5). The story of Christ to which Paul
appeals is a classic story of *praütēs*, the "gentle, disciplined calmness" of one who, "though he was in the form
of God, did not regard equality with God as something to
be exploited" (Philippians 2.6). This "gentle, disciplined
calmness" is the quality that the Bible—perhaps not surprisingly—links especially with those who exercise leadership among God's people. In the Old Testament, it is
associated specifically with Moses, and in the New, with
Paul, and, much more importantly, with Jesus Christ
himself. How specially appropriate it is, then, to those
who are called to leadership in the church!

The ancients perceived both "thinking soberly" and
"gentle, disciplined calmness" as aspects of "self-control"
(Greek, *egkrateia*) and "modesty" (Greek, *aidōs*—that is,
the "modesty" that arises from a proper sense of self and
a proper respect for others). It was not the case, as is
sometimes stated, that Paul's contemporaries did not

value emotions or pleasures, but they did think that full, mature human beings would be in control of these things, not they of them. This is a good deal of what is involved in the letter to the Ephesians, when the writer speaks of attaining to "maturity, to the measure of the full stature of Christ," of no longer being "tossed to and fro and blown about by every wind of doctrine" (Ephesians 4.13–14). No doubt "self-control" as an ideal, taken alone, had and has its limitations. Yet it remains a useful reminder to us that commitment to the church and to the world—commitment, in other words, to our baptismal vow to "respect the dignity of every human being"—is not simply a matter of good feelings or being a nice person. Still less is it a matter of "meeting my own needs," "creating my own reality," or "doing what's right for me." Commitment to respect the dignity of every human being demands of me that I attempt self-discipline, the surrender of my own will, and obedience. Not surprisingly, then, Paul regarded both "self-control" and "gentle, disciplined calmness" as fruits of the Spirit (see Galatians 5.23).

So much I would say about the character—the apostolic character—of those who are called to leadership in the house of God. What of the criteria that they might follow, when called to the act of decision-making? Certainly, if we take Paul seriously, two criteria will dominate. We have already mentioned them in connection with the fruits of Bible study. One is "edification," the "building up" of the body of Christ in love. The other is the church's "sanctification" (its "being made holy," "consecrated" as God's own)—which means God at work in it, claiming it for God's own, leading it to growth in the

Holy Spirit and in conformity with the person of Jesus Christ.

Evidently these two criteria so coincide in Paul's view as to be inseparable. So Paul pointed out to the Corinthians that as a community they had been "sanctified in Christ Jesus" (1 Corinthians 1.2). Concerned about their proneness to divisions and factions that could destroy their community, he reminded them that, as a church, God alone was the source of their life in Christ Jesus, "who became for us wisdom from God, and righteousness and sanctification and redemption" (1.30). Therefore they were God's planting, God's building (3.9), and, above all, they were God's temple.

> Do you not know that you are God's temple and that God's Spirit dwells in you? If anyone destroys God's temple, God will destroy that person. For God's temple is holy, and you are that temple. (1 Corinthians 3.16–17)

Whatever damages the body is an offense against God: this is the criterion by which the Corinthians should act.

> "All things are lawful," but not all things are beneficial. "All things are lawful," but not all things build up. Do not seek your own advantage, but that of the other.... So, whether you eat or drink, or whatever you do, do everything for the glory of God. Give no offense to Jews or to Greeks or to the church of God, just as I try to please[8] everyone in everything I do, not seeking my own advantage, but that of the many, so that they may be saved. Be imitators of me, as I am of Christ. (1 Corinthians 10:23–24, 31–11:1)

In the same spirit Paul wrote to the Christians at Rome:

> Let us therefore no longer pass judgment on one anoth-
> er, but resolve instead never to put a stumbling block or
> hindrance in the way of another. I know and am per-
> suaded in the Lord Jesus that nothing is unclean in
> itself; but it is unclean for anyone who thinks it unclean.
> (Romans 14.13–14)

The situation over observance of the Jewish law that
divided traditionalists and non-traditionalists at Rome
was a matter of rivalry among various groups, and Paul
applied his strictures to it, not because the question in
itself was important (Paul evidently thought it was not),
but because not to care for another's concerns was to
deny the spirit of the gospel, wherein "one died for all."

> If your brother or sister is being injured by what you eat,
> you are no longer walking in love. Do not let what you
> eat cause the ruin of one for whom Christ died. So do
> not let your good be spoken of as evil.... Let us then
> pursue what makes for peace and for mutual upbuild-
> ing. (Romans 14.15–16, 19)

The point is this: the issue for Paul is always the good
of the church—not, let it be stressed, the future church,
the eschatological church, the perfect church of some
unknown future, but the church *now*, the messy, scruffy,
struggling, confused, half-baked pilgrim people who are
to be found in Corinth or Philippi or Rome or wherever
at this precise moment. Therefore the important question for Paul in any dispute will always be, *not* "Does what
I am doing, or propose to do, meet my personal needs?"
or "Does it fit with my understanding of the kingdom?"
or "Does it sit well with my conscience?" but rather "Does
it serve to build up the community in Christ, or to break
it down? Does it help strengthen my brothers and sisters,

or make them weaker? Does it lead to the church's growth in holiness, or not?"

> We who are strong ought to put up with the failings of the week, and not to please ourselves. Each of us must please our neighbor for the good purpose of building up the neighbor. (Romans 15.1–2)

Why should those who follow Christ exercise this restraint? Because that is the nature of the one who is their Lord and to whom they belong, "For Christ did not please himself" (15.3). Therefore,

> put away from you all bitterness and wrath and anger and wrangling and slander, together with all malice, and be kind to one another, tenderhearted, forgiving one another, as God in Christ has forgiven you. (Ephesians 4.31–32)

There is a sense in which the church is an egalitarian society, but, as Paul also makes clear, that equality is before God and in Christ (Galatians 3.28). Therefore the church is not a monarchy, or an oligarchy, or a democracy. The church is a theocracy. Its existence stands or falls with the fact that it seeks to obey as the apostles and prophets sought to obey. It stands or falls by an absolute and irreversible distinction between ourselves and God's revelation, in which we receive, learn, and joyfully submit, thereby, like Mary, finding our fullness and our destiny, in which we have a Lord and belong to our Lord utterly, even as Paul was proud to be "the slave of Jesus Christ" (see Romans 1.1).

When therefore the church is true to its calling, it seeks to be guided neither by the will of the majority, nor by its own consensus, but by the will of God. The will of the majority may, after all, be mistaken. Consensus may be mistaken. General councils have erred. Only the Holy Spirit is promised to guide us "into all truth," because, as Jesus reminds us, only the Holy Spirit "will not speak on his own, but will speak whatever he hears, and he will declare to you the things that are to come. He will glorify me, because he will take what is mine and declare it to you" (John 16.13–14).

But what are we to do when we cannot agree over issues that seem to us to be significant? When what seems to us the obvious way to be faithful to the scriptures and to obey God is not so seen by others who are also believers, and who also have consciences?[9]

To begin with, so as long as we can recognize that those with whom we disagree are nonetheless struggling with the same issues of faithfulness and obedience as we are, we *must* try to go on talking with them, so as not to divide the body. That does not mean, of course, that we can be sure that we will agree with each other, but it does point to a good reason why we must always be hesitant in our disagreements and listen carefully to each other, exercising, according to the apostolic model, a "gentle, disciplined calmness" and "sober thinking." Just why might these people's opinions (these people with whom I find myself in such utter disagreement!) yet be a word of God's Spirit to the church? Merely to raise such a question means that we have much listening and thinking to do, even if we still cannot understand or agree.

If others arrive at moral judgments that are different from ours, and yet we still recognize them as members of Christ's people, this leaves our own moral judgments to some extent in doubt. We cannot be sure that ours is the only conceivable understanding of the faith. On the other hand, if we *are* sure that the others are wrong, then our remaining in communion with them means that we accept for ourselves the woundedness and sinfulness in the church that this involves. That is why it is so important that when we confess our sins at the liturgy we confess them both as individuals and also *as a body.* We do not (as we do when we make our personal confession in the presence of a priest) simply say, "I accuse myself" but "we have sinned." So the church's need for healing and mercy is bound up with our own individual needs for healing and mercy—and it is, I hope, hardly necessary to say that these are never things that we can gain by our own efforts. We receive them from God alone, for, as Paul repeatedly reminds us, it is by God's justice and mercy alone that we stand. So we must end where we began: remembering that it is God alone who is the source of our life in Christ Jesus (1 Corinthians 1.30).

It is deeply distressing to me, even when a cause that I support seems to "win" in the councils of the church, if I see that "victory" accompanied by a refusal on the part of the "victors" to sympathize with the defeated, by a lack of concern for their pain, and even by a crowing over them, as if they were no longer our brothers or our sisters. Such an attitude seems very far indeed from that of the apostle: "Who is weak, and I am not weak? Who is made to stumble, and I am not indignant?" (2 Corinthians 11.29). It is also very far from our understanding of God as one who "desires everyone to be saved and to come to the knowledge of the truth" (1 Timothy 2.4). All this is even more distressing when our crowing is accompanied in other contexts by our criticism of "triumphalism" in the church. "Triumphalism" is, it seems, always something of which others are guilty, never we ourselves.

We need always to bear in mind that the New Testament does not speak of salvation as an event wherein we will be victorious and everyone else will have to become like us. Salvation in the New Testament means that Christ will be victorious, and that God will be all in all. Any victory that we have will be God's gift to us, through our Lord Jesus Christ. And this will be so. God is not mocked. No Christianity can call itself biblical if it does not accept that God's plan will be fulfilled, and that in connection with God's plan all human action, even the obedience of the saints, is contingent—infinitely precious in God's sight, but contingent, nonetheless.

In the meantime, it is always possible that in matters that divide us both we and our opponents have a part of the truth (even though we cannot yet see it), and if we ignore each other or (even worse) separate from each other, instead of listening to each other and praying together, we shall each be in danger of losing the other's truth. Earlier I noted that after four hundred years the Roman Catholic Church and the Lutherans have finally agreed on a statement about justification. Neither the insights of the Reformation nor those of the Counter-Reformation appear to have been surrendered. But why did it take four hundred years to reach this understanding? Partly, no doubt, because the question was difficult, but also because of sin. More precisely, because what should have been matter for prayer and listening to the other became instead the rallying cry of parties and factions, and the tool of politicians and power-seekers. Had the original reformers and counter-reformers listened to each other more, prayed together more, and talked past each other less—had they, to put it another way, displayed more of the qualities of "sober thinking" and "gentle, disciplined calmness," undoubtedly these under-standings could have been reached sooner, and we—all of us, Roman Catholics and non-Roman Catholics alike—would not be heirs to the devastation they created out of the western church.

Where then does this leave us? It leaves us where we always were, with no resource but God, and no way to turn to God but in prayer—prayer, which is the Holy Spirit's work in us; prayer, which can finally be for nothing else than a peace and a unity that are quite beyond our present ability to grasp or understand. That peace and that unity are our challenge, our destiny, and God's promise to us.

> Lord Jesus Christ, you said to your apostles, "Peace I give to you; my own peace I leave with you": Regard not our sins, but the faith of your Church, and grant to us the peace and unity of that heavenly City, where with the Father and the Holy Spirit you live and reign, one God, now and for ever. Amen.

Notes

1. Deirdre J. Good, Jesus the Meek King (Harrisburg: Trinity Press International, 1999).

2. Plato, Phaedo 115d-117a, trans. Hugh Tredennick.

3. The Greek praos is the adjective cognate with praütēs.

4. Isocrates, To Nicocles 23.

5. See, for example, Josephus, Jewish War 350, 383.

6. Good, Jesus the Meek King, 8. To be fair to the translators of the King James and Douay-Rheims versions, "meek" in the early seventeenth century was actually a much better translation of the Greek praus (and Latin mansuetus) than it is now, since in addition to meaning "free from haughtiness and self-will" and "patient and unresentful under

injury or reproach," it also carried the (now obsolete) senses of "courteous," "kind," and, when used of someone in a superior position, "merciful," "compassionate," and even "indulgent," (see the definitions for "meek" in the *Oxford English Dictionary 2*). Thus, when Shakespeare's Mark Anthony says, "I am meek and gentle with these butchers," he is certainly not saying that he is submitting to those who have killed Caesar, but rather that, as a means to an end, he is for the moment staying calm and being polite to them *(Julius Caesar* III.i.255).

7. "Fools" (Greek, *a-phronoi*) are, we may note, virtually by definition those who do not have *sōphrosunē*—discretion, moderation, or prudence!

8. "Try to please" translates the Greek verb *areskō* that could be used in a positive sense (as here), or a negative one. In a positive sense it frequently carries the sense of accommodating others by meeting their needs or carrying out important obligations.

9. In what follows, I dare say that my indebtedness to Rowan Williams is obvious. See in particular his "On Making Moral Decisions," in *Sewanee Theological Review* 42.2 (1999): 155.

Four Notes

Note 1: The Rule of Faith

I use the expression "the rule of faith" (Latin, *regula fidei,* Greek, *kanōn pisteōs*) in more or less the sense in which it was used by the church fathers, Tertullian and Irenaeus, although the latter also favors other phrases such as the rule (or canon) "of the truth." The rule of faith for them does not refer to a formal creed—the creeds, like the canon of scripture itself, were still in the process of formulation—but rather to the general sense, outline, and essence of the revelatory story as it was told everywhere by the people of God and had been told from the beginning. When Tertullian and Irenaeus cite the rule of faith, it is clear that they perceive this universality as a mark of its authority. They also understand it as enshrining the central truths about the Father, the Son, and the Holy Spirit, and about the life, death, and resurrection of Jesus Christ. So, for example, Irenaeus in his *Proof of the Apostolic Preaching,* composed at Lyons (where he was bishop) late in the second or early in the third century:

We must keep strictly, without deviation, the rule of
faith, and carry out the commands of God, believing in
God, and fearing him, because he is Lord, and loving
him, because he is Father.... And this is the drawing up
of our faith, the foundation of the building, and the
consolidation of a way of life. God, the Father, uncreat-
ed, beyond grasp, invisible, one God the maker of all;
this is the first and foremost article of our faith.
But the second article is the Word of God, the Son of
God, Christ Jesus our Lord, who was shown forth by the
prophets according to the design of their prophecy and
according to the manner in which the Father disposed;
and through him were made all things whatsoever. He
also, in the end of times, for the recapitulation of all
things, is become a man among men, visible and tangi-
ble, in order to abolish death and bring to light life, and
bring about the communion of God and humankind.
And the third article is the Holy Spirit, through whom
the prophets prophesied and the patriarchs were taught
about God and the just were led in the paths of justice,
and who in the end of times has been poured forth in a
new manner upon humanity over all the earth renewing
humankind to God. (3.6 transl. Joseph E. Smith)

Both Irenaeus and Tertullian believed that the scriptures *as a whole* witnessed to the rule of faith, and that
this witness would be clear when the scriptures were read
as a whole. Indeed, Irenaeus' *Proof* is in its entirety essentially an argument for this claim (see also Tertullian's
Against Praxeas 26). On the other hand, Tertullian was
certainly aware that heretics could interpret parts of the
scriptures to support their own views, and sees the rule of
faith as a source of guidance toward correct interpretation (*de Praescriptione Haereticorum* 19).

Note 2: All Things Necessary to Salvation
"Holy Scripture containeth all things necessary to salvation *(Scriptura sacra continet omnia, quae ad salutem sunt
necessaria),*" affirms Article VI of The Thirty-Nine
Articles (*BCP* 868). It has been suggested to me by a not
unfriendly critic that my appeal in Chapter One to Article
VI strains the sense that the phrase "necessary to salvation" can be expected to bear. In response, I point to no
less an Anglican authority than the seventeenth-century
divine Richard Hooker, who was certainly nearer to the
rhetoric of 1571 (when the articles were first drafted)
than any modern critic can hope to be, and who, in his
Laws of Ecclesiastical Polity, appears to have understood
"necessary to salvation" in exactly the sense in which I
interpret it:

> Albeit Scripture do profess to contain in it all things that
> are necessary unto salvation, yet the meaning cannot be
> simply of all things which are necessary, but all things
> that are necessary in some certain kind or form, as all
> things which are necessary, and either could not at all or
> could not easily be known by the light of natural dis-
> course. . . . The main drift of the whole New Testament is
> that which St. John setteth down as the purpose of his
> own history, These things are written, that ye might
> believe that Jesus is Christ the Son of God, and that in
> believing ye might have life through His Name. The
> drift of the Old that which the Apostle mentioneth to
> Timothy, The Holy Scriptures are able to make thee wise
> unto salvation. So that the general end both of Old and
> New is one: the difference between them consisting in
> this, that the Old did make wise by teaching salvation
> through Christ that should come, the New by teaching
> that Christ the Savior is come, and that Jesus whom they

did crucify, and whom God did raise again from the dead, is He.

Obviously relevant here is a suggestion made by Paul Ricoeur, that biblical narratives fall into a category of narrative wherein "the ideological interpretation these narratives wish to convey is not superimposed on the narrative by the narrator, but is, instead, incorporated into the very strategy of the narrative.... Simply as a narrative, it exercises an interpretive function."[1]

Note 3: Literary Judgments and Literal Sense
Kevin Vanhoozer, an evangelical scholar, has suggested that the Vatican declaration on Divine Revelation

> errs in viewing the Bible as a single type of literature unified by its overarching salvific purpose.... The distinctive elements of the various literary genres are by and large smoothed over to make a seamless canon that is efficacious to God's saving purpose and that thus enjoys "saving" truth.[2]

While I agree with Vanhoozer that awareness of the different genres and styles of literature in the Bible is an important factor in understanding it, nonetheless I see no reason in this respect to support his criticism of the Vatican declaration. The declaration goes on in its next section to make very clear statements about the importance of paying attention to the various literary forms of Holy Scripture, as well as to matters of social and literary convention, if we are to determine "the intention of the sacred writers." What the declaration does then also point out is that perceived differences of style, genre, and so on should not blind us to "the content and unity of the whole of Scripture, taking into account the Tradition of

the entire church." The balance thus proposed between
an awareness of biblical diversity and an equal awareness
of what binds the biblical texts together—both being
matters of sound literary judgment—appears to me be
exactly right. These in turn are correctly distinguished
from the question of inerrancy, which is a theological
question, and a matter of faith.

Nevertheless, in drawing attention to our need, if we
are to interpret soundly, to identify the different types of
literature and genre in the Bible, Vanhoozer reminds us of
something important. That the Bible is dominated by
what Irenaeus called "the rule of faith," is, I insist, a literary conclusion, a conclusion based on the nature and
content of the Bible as a collection of written texts. By
contrast, it is a supreme error to insist that all scripture
must be taken "literally"—meaning that the texts must
always be taken to be offering us *objective* truth, as in a
piece of scientific, factually accurate reporting. Those
who do so are not taking the texts "literally" in the normal sense of that word: that is to say, they are not interpreting the texts by taking the words and expressions they
contain in their natural or customary meanings (which
of course means their natural or customary meanings in
the contexts in which they occur), and applying the ordinary rules of grammar. Such, for example, are those who
insist on the factual historicity of the books of Jonah and
Daniel, despite the fact that for anyone with any sense of
literature at all (and in marked contrast to, say, the court
histories of Saul and David or the descriptions of Paul's
journeys in Acts) the books of Jonah and Daniel scream
"fable" in every detail of style, ethos, and content. They
are, of course, very striking fables. They are prophetic
fables with insights that Jesus himself used as means to

express his message and the hope that he brought. At times they are very funny fables (especially Jonah—think of the conclusion!). But they are fables, nonetheless, and no whit the worse or the less because of that. God spoke to our ancestors through the prophets, the writer to the Hebrews says, "in many and various ways" (1.1), and this just happens to be one of them.

If those who insist on the historical accuracy of Jonah and Daniel were truly to take these texts *literally*, that is, *as literature*, they would be sensitive to the kinds of text with which they were dealing, and the modes in which those texts seek to convey whatever it is they seek to convey. Then they would not make the mistake of imposing upon them criteria of historical accuracy that in terms of any (in the normal sense) "literal" approach to them are obviously not appropriate.

I am aware that the historicity of the book of Jonah is sometimes defended on the grounds that "Jesus affirmed it, and therefore it must be so."[3] Regardless of the faulty theology implied by the conclusion to that particular argument, it ought to be pointed out that, as regards what we can learn from the evangelists' testimony, even the premise is not well founded. Jesus' words about his own future based on the book of Jonah (Matthew 12.39–41and Luke 11.29–32, Matthew 16.4) appear in their rhetoric to be (with all respect) exactly similar to the way in which when I was young my parents used another story to warn me against fibbing. "You know what happened to Pinocchio!" they said. I took their point. There was no need to unwrap it or spell it out. But that did not mean that even at nine years old I was daft enough to imagine that the story of Pinocchio was meant to be "true" in the way that the stories of Julius Caesar and

William the Conqueror in my history books were meant to be "true"—and I am perfectly sure that my parents did not think I was. Only those who are first willing to see the scriptures as they are, as words, as texts that use different genres and styles—only those who acknowledge all that, and then acknowledge the "something of great constancy," the golden thread that is nonetheless the scriptures' evident *raison d'être* as a collection of texts, only those who do both those things can be said to be reading the scriptures "literally."

It may be that we should think of most "literalists" simply as literalists in the rather sad sense in which we use the word to speak of those who do not understand a piece of irony, or a joke, or a beautiful poem, because they do not understand the kinds of words they are hearing. ("But just *why* did the chicken want to get to the other side?") They, as we say, "just don't get it." Their views are of course simplistic nonsense. But then, in justice to them, we should confess that we all have moments when we are tempted to yield to the seductions of the simplistic, with its appearance of easy rationality, rather than face the often harsh and much more complicated challenges posed by the truth.

Note 4: Preferring the More Difficult Reading
In Chapter Seven, I discuss briefly the phenomenon of apparent "factual inaccuracies" in the Bible. Examples of these were the incorrect dating of David's eating the bread from the Temple (Mark 2.26), and the misattribution of a passage from the prophets (Matthew 27.9). Another, and very well known, example of misattributed prophecy would be Mark's attribution to Isaiah of what appears to be a combination of allusions to various

prophetic texts (see Mark 1.2-3 in the RSV, NRSV, or
NAB). In respect of all three passages, manuscripts have
come down to us from antiquity that appear to say what
is "correct," and other manuscripts have come down to us
that appear to be in "error," although the "correct" versions of Mark 2.26 and Matthew 27.9 have not had the
widespread effect on the manuscript tradition as a whole
that the "correct" version of Mark 1.2 had (see the King
James Version). In all three cases, however, the textual
scholars incline to believe that the "erroneous" text is likely to be the more original.[4]

Why? Is this mere perverseness on their part, or simply
"Enlightenment skepticism"? It is neither. The textual
scholars are following a principle of textual comparison
that was enunciated by no less a doctor of the church than
Augustine of Hippo: the principle of preferring the more
difficult reading. Thus, with regard to the problem of
Matthew 27.9, where the evangelist attributes to Jeremiah
a verse that appears to come from Zechariah 11.13,
Augustine pointed out that some manuscripts avoided the
problem by stating simply that the words that Matthew
quoted came from "the prophet." He noted that it would
be possible to say that those manuscripts deserved to be
followed at this point, rather than those that attributed
the quotation to Jeremiah. But then, with admirable
frankness, Augustine went on to admit that he was not
really satisfied with this solution. He pointed out that "a
majority of manuscripts contain the name of Jeremiah,
and those who have studied the Gospel with more than
usual care in the Greek copies report that they have found
it to stand so in the more ancient Greek exemplars." He
then proceeded, in effect, to articulate the critical rule that
"the more difficult reading is to be preferred":

I look also to this further consideration, namely that there was no reason why this name should have been added and a corruption thus created; whereas there was certainly an intelligible reason for erasing the name from so many of the manuscripts. For presumptuous inexperience *(audax imperitia)* might readily have done that, when perplexed with the problem presented by the circumstance that this passage cannot be found in Jeremiah.[5]

Modern scholars follow the same reasoning with regard to Mark 1.2 and 2.26. Thus, with regard to the former, Metzger writes,

> The quotation in verses 2 and 3 is composite, the first part being from Mal. 3.1 and the second part from Is. 40.3. It is easy to see, therefore, why copyists should have altered the words "in Isaiah the prophet" (a reading found in the earliest representative witnesses of the Alexandrian, the Western, and the Caesarean types of text) to the more comprehensive introductory formula "in the prophets."[6]

By contrast, it is much harder to see why anyone would have wanted to change the perfectly straightforward "in the prophets" to the obviously problematic "in the prophet Isaiah."

This entire discussion is an example of what scholars of an earlier generation used to call "lower criticism," not because they thought it inferior to other kinds of biblical study, but because one had to do it first as a foundation for the other kinds. Modern scholars usually refer to it as "textual criticism." It is the study and evaluation of the various manuscripts of the New Testament that have come down to us from antiquity, in order to try to arrive at the "best text," that is, the text most likely to be closest to the "autograph" (what the original author actually wrote or dictated—a notion, it should be pointed out, that is in itself not without problems).

Textual criticism is fascinating to people who think in a certain way, especially those who like detection and enjoy spending a lot of time on details. The problem that faces the New Testament textual critic is that there exist thousands of manuscripts of the New Testament from the era before the use of printing, and they do not all say the same thing. While these variations do not affect any point of Christian faith or practice, still the variations exist. Sometimes they are very interesting, and at least some people are interested in the problem of trying to understand and evaluate them.

Notes

1. Paul Ricoeur, "Interpretative Narrative," trans. David Pellauer, in *The Book and the Text: The Bible and Literary Theory,* ed. Regina M. Schwarz (Oxford: Basil Blackwell, 1990), 237.

2. Kevin J. Vanhoozer, "The Semantics of Biblical Literature: Truth and Scripture's Diverse Literary Forms," in *Hermeneutics, Authority, and Canon,* ed. D. A. Carson and John D. Woodbridge (Carlisle: Paternoster Press, 1995), 102.

3. So, essentially, Harold Lindsell, *Battle for the Bible* (Grand Rapids: Zondervan, 1976), 21.

4. See, for example, Bruce M. Metzger, *Textual Commentary on the Greek New Testament: A Companion Volume to the United Bible Societies' Greek New Testament,* third edition (London and New York: United Bible Societies, 1975 [corrected]), 66, 73, and 79.

5. Augustine, *De Consensu Evangel* 3.7.29, cited in Bruce M. Metzger, *The Text of the New Testament: Its Transmission, Corruption, and Restoration,* third edition, enlarged (New York and Oxford: Oxford University Press, 1992), 153–54.

6. Metzger, *Textual Commentary,* 73.

Suggestions for Further Reading

Among general studies by individual scholars, I am especially indebted to Paul J. Achtemeier, *Inspiration and Authority: Nature and Function of Christian Scripture* (Peabody, Mass.: Hendrickson, 1999); and Sandra M. Schneiders, *The Revelatory Text: Interpreting the New Testament as Sacred Scripture,* second edition (Collegeville, Minn.: The Liturgical Press, 1999). From a specifically Anglican viewpoint, the following, though both quite short, are jewels: Arthur Michael Ramsey, "The Authority of the Bible" in *Peake's Commentary on the Bible,* ed. Matthew Black and H. H. Rowley (London: Thomas Nelson, 1962), 1–7; and Reginald H. Fuller, "Authority and Method: Scripture," in *The Study of Anglicanism,* ed. Stephen Sykes and John Booty (London: SPCK / Philadelphia: Fortress, 1998), 79–91.

For those who wish to consider scripture from the viewpoint of systematic theologians, I would suggest starting with Karl Rahner, *Foundations of Christian Faith:*

An Introduction to the Idea of Christianity, trans. William
V. Dych (New York: Crossroad, 1985), 361–65, 369–78
(writing from a Roman Catholic perspective), and Robert
W. Jenson, *Systematic Theology,* vol. 2 (New York: Oxford
University Press, 1999), 270–84 (writing from a
Reformation perspective). It is surprising—and agreeable
to the ecumenically minded—to note the extent to which
the two approaches complement each other.

Those who are interested in the "four senses" of scripture should investigate Henri de Lubac's *Medieval
Exegesis,* vol. 1, *The Four Senses of Scripture,* trans. Mark
Sewbanc (Grand Rapids: William B. Eerdmans /
Edinburgh: T. & T. Clark, 1998). This is a great, sprawling,
untidy book that would have benefited from sensitive
editing; it is also an enormous depository of wisdom and
information, wherein treasures abound. It is unfortunate
that a number of biblical scholars have seen in de Lubac's
work an attempt to retreat into past approaches to the
Bible, abandoning the fruits of scientific exegesis.[1] This is
quite to misunderstand it. De Lubac does not reject scientific exegesis any more than I do; nor does he encourage slavish imitation of patristic and medieval critics.
What he does ask is that modern biblical criticism
remember the concerns that led to the creation and
preservation of the Bible in the first place: questions
about the nature of life, the world, and existence. He does
not abandon scientific exegesis, but asks that scientific
exegesis remember its proper foundation, which is
Christian faith.

Among official and semi-official pronouncements by
the churches, I have over the years found the *Dogmatic
Constitution on Divine Revelation (Dei Verbum) of the
Second Vatican Council*[2] very helpful, as well as the rele-

vant sections of *Anglicans and Roman Catholics: The Search for Unity,* edited by Christopher Hill and Edward Yarnold, S. J. (London: SPCK / CTS, 1994).[3] Both repay study and reflection. Although somewhat dated, also still useful are the relevant sections of that by now classic statement by the Archbishops' Commission on Doctrine, *Doctrine in the Church of England: The Report of the Commission on Christian Doctrine appointed by the Archbishops of Canterbury and York in 1922* (London: SPCK, 1938).

Notes

1. For example, Joseph A. Fitzmyer, S.J., "The Senses of Scripture Today" in *Irish Theological Quarterly* 62 (1996-97): 114.

2. This document was published on 18 November, 1965, and may be found in *Vatican Council II: The Conciliar and Post Conciliar Documents,* ed. Austin Flannery, O.P. (Collegeville, Minn.: Liturgical Press, 1974), 750–65. Also invaluable as background to the *Constitution* is the *Commentary on the Documents of Vatican II,* ed. Herbert Vorgrimler, vol. 3 (New York and London: Herder and Herder, 1969), 155–272.

3. In view of the confused reception that these reports received, not only among Anglicans but also among Roman Catholics, it is hard to know quite how the ARCIC documents should be categorized in terms of their standing with the churches. But they have at least the authority of the very weighty group of Anglican and Roman Catholic theologians that produced them, and that in itself is not something to be regarded lightly. My suspicion is that the ARCIC documents will eventually be seen as having been chiefly at fault in being somewhat ahead of their time.